NOTHING LESS

Nothing less than the whole Bible can make a whole Christian.

-A.W. TOZER

© 2017 LifeWay Christian Resources.

November 2017 Reprint

Item 005799608

ISBN 978-1-4627-8023-5

Published by LifeWay Christian Resources, One LifeWay Plaza, Nashville, TN 37234

For ordering or inquiries, visit *www.lifeway.com*, or write LifeWay Resources Customer Service, One LifeWay Plaza, Nashville, TN 37234-0113.

We believe that the Bible has God for its author; salvation for its end; and truth, without any mixture of error, for its matter and that all Scripture is totally true and trustworthy. To review LifeWay's doctrinal guideline, please visit *lifeway.com/doctrinalguideline*.

FOREWORD

As a ministry leader you spend countless hours thinking, planning, meeting, and dreaming about the spiritual transformation of the people you lead. It never leaves your mind. And it shouldn't because you have the privilege of leading the next generation during their most formative stage: childhood. In partnership with parents, teachers, and other leaders, you will have a profound impact on the lives of the children sitting in the chairs of your church each week. And so the question "Is my children's ministry focused on the right thing?" is an important one. Unfortunately, many ministries ask this question only in terms of organization and programming.

Based on research and ministry expertise, Jana Magruder tackles this question head-on. Her insight as a mom, educator, and former children's ministry leader will help you discover the one thing that's needed in children's ministry above everything else. Her book is practical, helpful, and will challenge your current thinking in children's ministry. What I especially love about *Nothing Less* is how it can equip you, the children's ministry leader, to enable parents to fulfill their role as the primary discipler.

I've had the pleasure of serving with Jana Magruder for the last four years here at LifeWay. I can attest to her passion for serving local church leaders in an effort to help them establish healthy children's ministries that partner well with the home. Simply put, this book will help you minister more effectively to the children and parents in your church, and it will challenge parents to take their calling as the primary discipler more seriously.

Ben Trueblood
Director of Student Ministry, LifeWay Christian Resources

ABOUT THE AUTHOR

Jana Magruder serves as the Director of Kids Ministry for LifeWay Christian Resources and brings a wealth of experience and passion for ministry, education, and publishing trustworthy content. A graduate of Baylor University and a native Texan, she has written award-winning curricula, both interactive and traditional in nature, for the state of Texas, IMAX films, and international authors, as well as churches and ministries. She is also the author of *Kids Ministry that Nourishes* and *Life Verse Creative Journal*, which she co-wrote with her daughter, Morgan Grace, for girls of all ages. In addition to their daughter, Jana and her husband, Michael, have two boys and reside in Nashville, Tennessee.

Dedication from Jana: With fresh conviction, I dedicate this book to my family. *Nothing Less* has taught me that no matter how hard I may try to make spiritual development about all the other things, God has made it very simple—His Word is the way. Let's dig in together.

ABOUT THE DESIGNER

Stephanie Salvatore serves as the Graphic Design Specialist for LifeWay Kids, leading the team of designers that creates award-winning work for Vacation Bible School, kids curriculum, magazines, and events. Stephanie has a passion for collaborating with writers and editors, seeking out that sweet spot where the written word and the graphic design come together in a brilliant spark that delights and communicates. She teaches 2nd-3rd grade girls Sunday School as well as serving as a Kids Ministry coach at her church. Stephanie, Joe, and their children, Ben and Chloe, live in Nashville, Tennessee.

Dedication from Stephanie: For Ben and Chloe. How thankful I am that God chose me to be your Mom. May God lavishly gift you with a love for His Word, such that nothing less ever satisfies you. I pray that you fall more and more in love with Him every day.

ACKNOWLEDGMENTS

This project has been a group effort that has spanned teams and departments at LifeWay and beyond. It's not by coincidence, however, that each of us who have poured into it are parents who truly share the same desire to know how to best influence our kids for the gospel during their most formidable years.

I want to first thank our designer, **Stephanie Salvatore**—mom of two, who is the most talented designer I have ever known. It's amazing to work with someone who can use her gift to share the gospel in such a powerful way. Most research books can put you to sleep by page two, but Stephanie won't have it that way. She uses her ability to curate content through visual depiction in the beautiful infographics, photographs, and graphical layout you will see on every page.

To **Scott McConnell**, a dad first and professional researcher second, who helped our team capture the vision of telling this story through solid statistical research.

Thank you to **Chuck Peters**, dad of four, who sat at the ideation table to help craft the content and hone the questions we needed to tell this convicting story.

And to **Dr. William Summey**, our amazing editor and publisher. William, dad of two, worked tirelessly to weave together the ultimate narrative of *Nothing Less*.

TABLE OF
CONTENTS

3 46 15 INFLUENCERS OF SPIRITUAL HEALTH

4 108 WHAT CAN PARENTS DO?

5 118 YOU CAN DO THIS!

INTRODUCTION

This book began with one question. What can I as a parent do to most highly influence my children to become spiritually healthy adults? I am constantly in awe of the men and women God placed in my life through the years, and sometimes I am audacious enough to say, "What in the world did your parents do to raise such an incredible Christ follower?" Restated, I began this research organically by asking a few people about their spiritual upbringing.

It turns out, that's not enough to publish statistically significant research that people can learn from and put into practice. So, our LifeWay Kids team partnered with the LifeWay Research team to officially find out the answer to my question. Together, we developed a survey that would ask Christian parents about their adult children. One question turned into many questions as we realized that we would like to know exactly what worked—and what did not. In other words, what parenting practices made a statistical impact on the spiritual health of these adult children?

Desperate to find a magic formula for my own mothering, I really wanted to know some specifics. Am I spending my time the right way? I know I am supposed to be the primary discipler of my children, but what does that really mean? I knew that if I felt this way, others shared my curiosity and urgency. I knew church leaders and ministry leaders to kids, students, and families would certainly want to know the results.

So, here it is. Encapsulated into a visual story that will help us all understand best practices for the spiritual development of kids and teens, but with one big take-away that smacks you in the face. It may not necessarily be a surprise, but it is truly convicting. Turn the page to discover why **Nothing Less** is more than we could have ever imagined.

Jana

ABOUT THE NOTHING LESS STUDY

Parents have a front-row seat for the fast-forward story of their children's lives. Yet they are also proactive players in the story, constantly thinking about the implications of their child's choices and trying to stay a step ahead to teach, warn, and protect. Much like Mary, parents treasure these things in their heart. The Nothing Less Research was a quest to unearth this treasure.

Our sample for this study was 2,000 Protestant adults who have finished the parenting journey with one or more kids ages 18-30 (children could include birth, step, adopted, or foster children). The parents didn't have to be near-perfect. They simply had to attend church once a month or more.

Quotas and weights ensured the targeted sample obtained from a national online panel demographically has the exact proportions as the full population. The survey was completed September 22–October 5, 2016.

Parents unlocked the treasures in their memories and hearts by describing their parenting practices, as well as characteristics and habits of their children "as they were growing up." We also asked them to describe 9 spiritual characteristics of their child today. Then we used statistical methods that identified 15 characteristics that predict their child's spiritual condition today.

The childhood characteristics that reveal differences in the spiritual condition of young adult children are unpacked in chapter 3. These influencers are not all equal. One has great impact, some moderate, and others smaller impact. Understanding the priorities for this journey is a gift from these parents that we now treasure.

Scott McConnell, *Executive Director, LifeWay Research*

2,000 parents of young adults were surveyed.

They evaluated each adult child's spiritual health ...

and answered questions about each child's upbringing.

15

This resulted in 15 characteristics that were predictive of spiritual health in adult children.

WE'RE ALL IN THE SAME BOAT

96 PERCENT OF PARENTS AGREE THEY CONSISTENTLY TRY TO BE BETTER PARENTS.

WE WANT TO BE BETTER PARENTS.

As parents, we have more in common than meets the eye—our trials and our triumphs, our routines and our limitations. Those commonalities often go undetected or unacknowledged. Once we begin recognizing our similar struggles and familiar frustrations, we can support one another in mutual, gospel-centered encouragement for the betterment of a healthy, happy home life. Although the particulars of our lives will vary from family to family, we are all, generally speaking, in the same boat. Because of this common situation, there is perhaps no surprise that research shows us that 96% of parents, at some level, agree with the statement "Parenting is a huge responsibility."[2]

Parenthood requires a balance of activity and reflection. Parents never stop learning how to be parents. We want the best for our kids. We invest endlessly in them as they grow. Whether they are learning to walk or are on the cusp of adulthood, we remain preoccupied with their development as well as with our own role as parents. We want to be good parents, and when we stop to think, we find that we want to be more than just good parents; we want to improve daily, waking up with the confidence that no matter what a new day may bring, we will know how to respond with understanding, grace, and maturity. We may want to be perfect. We may want our children to be perfect. But we can't be perfect, nor can our kids be perfect. It's normal for parents to have high, or even unrealistic, expectations for the realities of parenthood. But parenthood is a multifaceted responsibility. It calls for a constant commitment of time, resources, patience, consideration, and action. And a lot of love.

One of the most challenging parts of parenthood, especially as followers of Christ, is the knowledge that our children will be faced with hardships. We come to parenthood with decades of

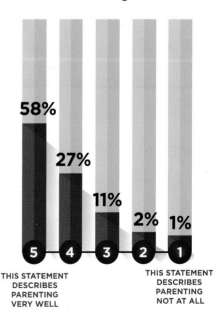

ALMOST ALL PARENTS agree with the statement "Parenting is a huge responsibility" to some degree.

58%

27%

11%

2% 1%

5 4 3 2 1

THIS STATEMENT DESCRIBES PARENTING VERY WELL

THIS STATEMENT DESCRIBES PARENTING NOT AT ALL

life-experience. Some of our experiences have been good. Others have been difficult. Moreover, the world of experience doesn't pause when we become parents; and in many ways, the realities of life's struggles only quicken as we—and our children—get older. We struggle to keep up with a culture that moves at an increasingly breakneck speed. We have good reason to feel uneasy at the prospect of our children's entrance into a tech-savvy world bursting with ingenuity, innovation, and distraction.

Let's consider a statistic that confirms this uneasiness. A sample of American parents were asked to react to the following prompt: When you think about what your children will face in the world when they become adults, you often feel fearful. In response to this prompt, 49% of respondents answered that they agree to an extent, and 33% percent said that they agree strongly. In contrast, only 18% of parents disagreed.[3] We can extract from this particular statistic a parental anxiety that is tangible. The data from this poll does not reflect a universal agreement that parents will fear for their children's place in the coming decades, but it does suggest that an overwhelming majority of parents worry about the world that awaits their kids.

At present, our country is perhaps less focused on Christ than ever, and this lack of attention manifests in the way young people drop away from church communities. What can we do to guide our children in the right direction? What should we do? We're all in the same boat, but where should we direct our sails?

82% OF PARENTS AGREE THAT "When you think about what your children will face in our world when they become adults, you often feel fearful."

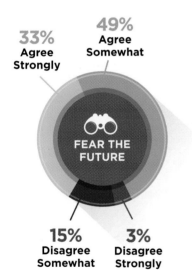

33% Agree Strongly

49% Agree Somewhat

FEAR THE FUTURE

15% Disagree Somewhat

3% Disagree Strongly

NOTHING LESS
       FOR THIS
     TINY LITTLE ONE
WHO HAS
       STOLEN MY HEART.

MOST AMERICANS AGREE ON WHAT IS MANDATORY TO BE A GOOD MOM OR DAD

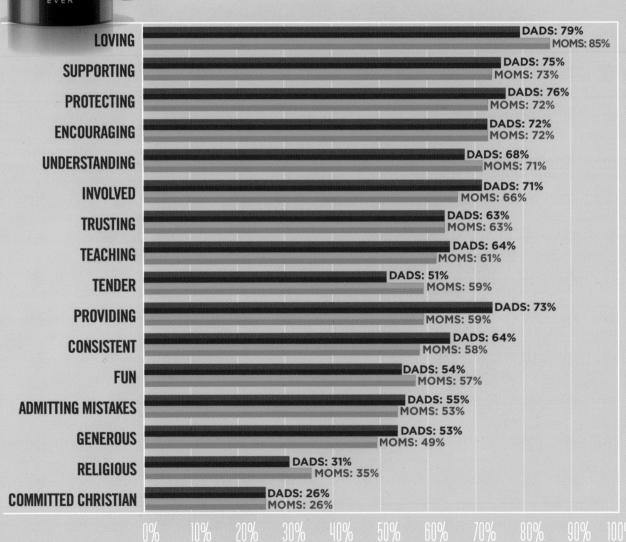

	DADS	MOMS
LOVING	79%	85%
SUPPORTING	75%	73%
PROTECTING	76%	72%
ENCOURAGING	72%	72%
UNDERSTANDING	68%	71%
INVOLVED	71%	66%
TRUSTING	63%	63%
TEACHING	64%	61%
TENDER	51%	59%
PROVIDING	73%	59%
CONSISTENT	64%	58%
FUN	54%	57%
ADMITTING MISTAKES	55%	53%
GENEROUS	53%	49%
RELIGIOUS	31%	35%
COMMITTED CHRISTIAN	26%	26%

0% 10% 20% 30% 40% 50% 60% 70% 80% 90% 100%

WHAT MAKES A GOOD PARENT?

What constitutes "good" parenting? Are there certain qualities that lead to being a "better" mom or dad? How do adults in the most "stable" families qualify their successes? Where does our Christian faith fit into the equation?

These are all relevant questions worthy of our attention. The truth, though, is that there is no cookie-cutter answer for these questions. There is no rough-and-ready template for achieving the distinction of "Master Parent." Good parenting practices must instead be cultivated. We may not all agree on what we choose to prioritize, but we must approach parenting with consistency. Good parents are fixed in their commitment to firmly held values and beliefs.

Look at the bar graph on the previous page. There you can see how many Americans define the mandatory requirements for good parenting. Take a moment to study the chart. Are there any items on the chart that you think should absolutely make the cut? Are there any items that you feel less strongly about? How do you feel about the muted response towards spirituality, or the almost 50/50 split concerning generosity? It is worth noting that this data represents an open sample of Americans.

Born-again evangelical Christians answered a little differently. These Christians were less likely to choose the categories Involved, Protecting, Supporting, Consistent, Understanding, or Fun than the population at large. On the other hand, Christian parents were much more likely to select Religious (47% in comparison), and those who chose Committed Christian doubled (51%) when compared to the general population. Faith and religious traditions are more important and, thus, shape a Christian parent.[4]

From this chart, though, we begin to see a widening gulf between families of faith and those who follow a social morality toward a

BORN-AGAIN EVANGELICAL CHRISTIANS DEFINE WHAT'S MANDATORY A LITTLE DIFFERENTLY.

THEY WERE LESS LIKELY TO SELECT:
Involved
Protecting
Supporting
Consistent
Understanding
Fun

THEY WERE MORE LIKELY TO SELECT:
Religious (47%)
Committed Christian (51%)

SECURITY IN GOD'S
UNCONDITIONAL
LOVE AND GRACE
GIVES DIRECTION
TO PARENTING
THAT IS ANCHORED
IN GOD'S
UNCHANGING
LOVE AND DOES
NOT SHIFT WITH
SOCIAL MORALITY
AND FASHIONABLE
TRENDS.

happy life. It is true that 85% want to be loving moms and 79% want to be loving dads. But toward what end? That end is the defining difference.

Parents in our society want their child to be independent, confident, and secure so they can be happy, successful, and fulfilled. Christian parents want their children to grow in a relationship with God and follow His plan for their lives, to worship and serve God above all else. Christian parents have security in God's unconditional love and grace toward them, out of which flows the love with which they parent. This certainty gives direction to parenting that is anchored in God's unchanging love and does not shift with social morality and fashionable trends.

But if these things are always the case, why don't evangelical Christians rank Committed Christian and Religious even higher in their view of what a good parent is? Let's look at the statistics on that trend.

"We are seeing an **ever-widening gulf** in American believers **between the private faith** and a faith that is **passed on.**

Instead we **too often** see an emphasis on guiding children to a **social morality** and toward an as-yet undefined **'happy'** life.**"**

–SCOTT MCCONNELL
EXECUTIVE DIRECTOR,
LIFEWAY RESEARCH

ONLY 29% SAY
FAITH
IS THE MOST IMPORTANT
INFLUENCE ON THEIR
PARENTING.

WHAT INFLUENCES PARENTS?

Only 29% of born-again Christians state that their personal faith plays the most significant role in their approach to parenting.[6] Twenty-nine seems like a pretty small percentage, doesn't it? It appears there is a temptation for many adult believers to keep separate or make a distinction between their relationship with God and their relationship with their children. The two are not naturally connected in the minds of these Christians. They may mean well in doing so. There may be crossover moments, where personal faith in Christ shine through their interactions with kids, but it does not regularly influence their parenting.

The Bible informs us that this approach — the approach in which belief and instruction are in relative isolation — is not the right one. In 2 Timothy, Paul addresses the difficulties of living life as followers of Christ in a dark and fallen world; yet Paul finds encouragement and, even more significantly, the strength to encourage his young disciple, Timothy, in his meditations on Scripture. Not just any Scripture, either, but the Scriptures he had known from a young age:

> *"Evil people and impostors will become worse, deceiving and being deceived. But as for you, continue in what you have learned and firmly believed. You know those who taught you, and you know that from infancy you have known the sacred Scriptures, which are able to give you wisdom for salvation through faith in Christ Jesus"* (2 Timothy 3:13-15).

It is worth noting that those who taught Timothy the sacred Scriptures are referred to by name, his mother Eunice and his grandmother, Lois (2 Timothy 1:3-5).

Our faith in the Lord and our calling as parents must be interdependent. We cannot assume that our children will make abstract connections between our parenting behaviors and our commitment

"WHEN SELF-IDENTIFYING CHRISTIANS ARE NOT ABLE TO SAY THAT FAITH IS A PRIORITY FOR PARENTING, WE SHOULD NOT BE SURPRISED AT THE PREVALENCE OF CHURCH DROPOUTS IN THE YOUNGER GENERATION."
-ED STETZER

to Christ. Therefore, we must strive daily to be bold, deliberate, and crystal-clear in how we let our faith and the Word of God inform our walk as parents. The more concrete this fusion of faith and parenting, the stronger our children will grow in their individual walks with the Father. The world is just as dark as it was in Paul's day—maybe even darker. Every new generation of children needs good parents, yes, but they also need the wisdom that can only come through the perfect instruction of our heavenly Parent, the Almighty God.

But the question remains: if not Scripture, where do Christians practically go for parenting advice?

WHERE DO PARENTS GO FOR ADVICE?

Wouldn't it be amazing if we knew the answers to life's many questions, if we could combat every new uncertainty with swift and easy poise? One of the ironies of the Information Age is that we're endlessly inundated with data, opinions, and news — but such a flexible connectivity can be utterly paralyzing! For every pearl of wisdom, there is an ocean of noise. There is simply too much out there for our minds to filter. We often don't know where we should turn for advice. We don't know who will listen, or who will understand.

We can devour book after book and browse blogs and websites, but the most valuable and time-tested source for parenting advice is the Bible. The Bible might be the most beloved and neglected book in America: 89% of households own a copy, and 41% of households own four or more copies,[6] but only 20% of Americans have read the Bible in its entirety. 23% have read only a few sentences or less of the Bible.[7] We will discuss this issue in more detail later as part of the research solutions. For many people, the Bible may as well be a

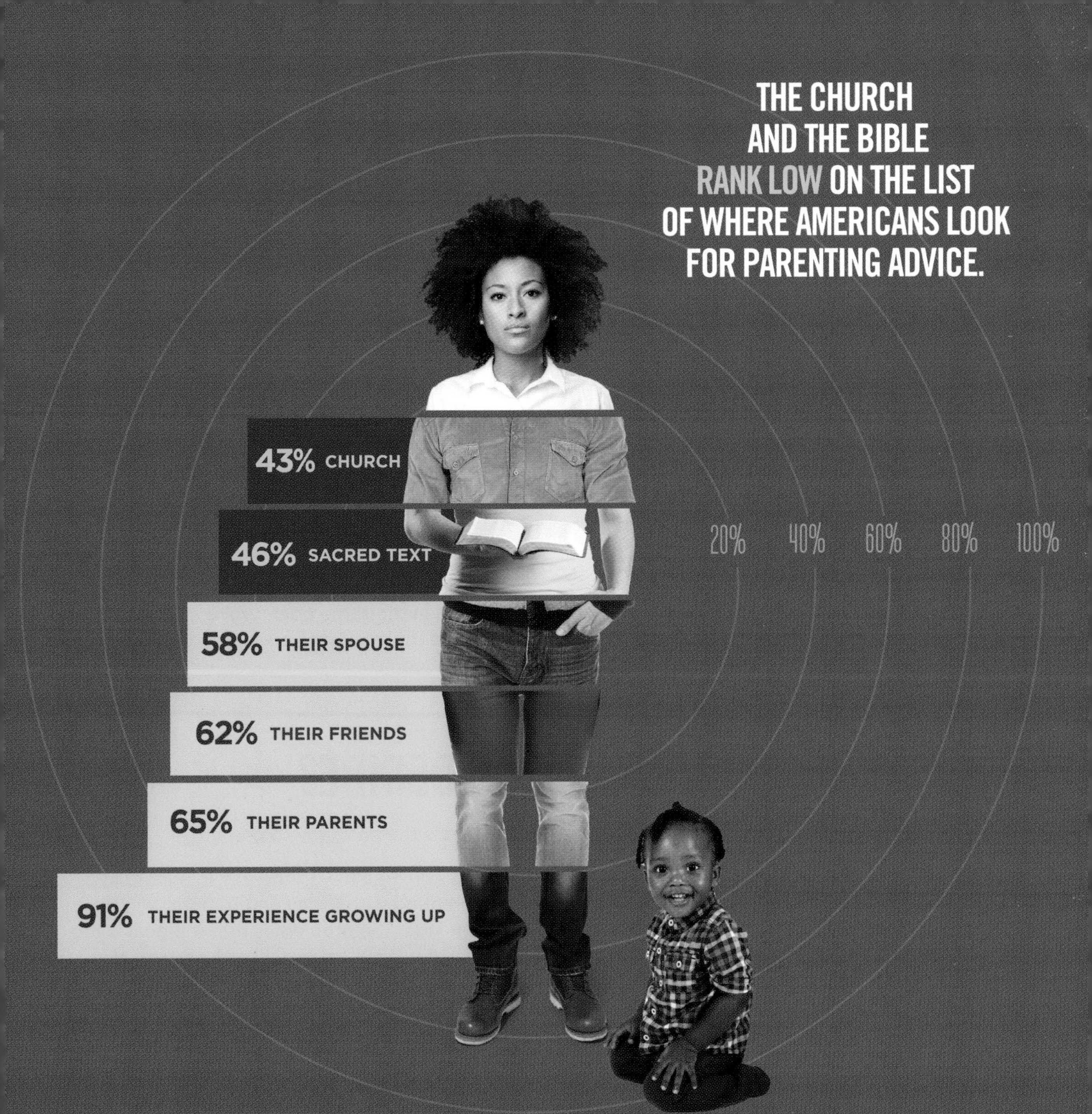

THE CHURCH
AND THE BIBLE
RANK LOW ON THE LIST
OF WHERE AMERICANS LOOK
FOR PARENTING ADVICE.

20%   40%   60%   80%   100%

43% CHURCH

46% SACRED TEXT

58% THEIR SPOUSE

62% THEIR FRIENDS

65% THEIR PARENTS

91% THEIR EXPERIENCE GROWING UP

collector's item. So where does the Bible rank on how it influences parents?

As you can see in the graphic to the left, only 14% of parents are aware of the Bible's efficacy as a parenting tool, even though 77% of parents identify as Christian. And whereas 91% of Americans look to their experience for parenting advice, only 46% look to the Bible for parenting advice, while even fewer turn to a church community.

Instead, parents largely depend on their experience growing up. Reflecting on their own upbringing, parents decide how they want to parent or how they don't want to continue a cycle of negative experiences from their upbringing. So, it is not surprising that almost two-thirds depend on their parents or friends to inform parenting decisions. A little more than half depend on a spouse. Less than half depend on the Bible or church in comparison.[8]

The truth is, if we study God's Word intently, we will find explicit and implicit advice that will bear positively on our ability to be godly parents. Remember, we're all in the same boat. We're all navigating unpredictable waters. Let the Bible inform your parenting and allow Christian community to come alongside you. Don't parent in isolation.

HOW DO YOU DECIDE?

So how do you decide what is the best way to parent?

Have you heard the expression, "Begin with the end in mind"? In some ways, we may be parenting with today and tomorrow in plain sight, striving to raise great kids. The problem is that the goal is too small and the vision too narrow. If we are really hard-pressed, we must admit that we don't want to raise great kids. We want to raise great adults who love and cherish God's Word.

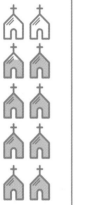

77%

While 77% of parents surveyed identify themselves as Christians ...

14%

only 14% are very familiar with what the Bible says about parenting.

The tiny humans that God has entrusted to us won't stay tiny forever. We'll all continue remarking year after year about how our kids are growing up too fast. There will definitely be moments when it feels that way. Growing up, however, is so much more than how tall they are, what level of math they can do, what games they no longer play, and how many pairs of shoes they can barely squeeze into anymore. Physically, our children are going to grow into adults; it is an inevitable fact of life that we can neither stop or slow. What is not guaranteed is the type of adult they grow to become.

The purpose of the research exposed and explained in this book is to help us cast a grand vision. What if we all parented our children with the end in mind? What if we made decisions based on what was best for their long-term spiritual development and not their immediate compliance or happiness? What if we focused less on 10 minutes from now and 10 days from now and really zeroed in on the type of adults we wanted to call our grown children 10 years from now? That's parenting with the end, not the moment, in mind.

The characteristics proven to have significant lasting impact in this study might just lead us to take steps toward encouraging these characteristics. We might just be able to help raise spiritually healthy adults who love God, follow Jesus, and walk in the power of the Spirit. Spoiler alert: Along the way, we'll be reminded over and over again that the work we do to fulfill our call as godly parents won't be nearly enough. Ultimately, we'll learn that trusting God for the end result we desire is really the only way to go.

THE PURPOSE OF THE NOTHING LESS RESEARCH EXPOSED AND EXPLAINED IN THIS BOOK IS TO HELP US CAST A GRAND VISION. WHAT IF WE ALL PARENTED OUR CHILDREN WITH THE END IN MIND?

WE'RE CHASING THE WRONG THINGS

HOW PARENTS DEFINE GOOD PARENTING

How do we define good parenting? Or to put the question in a more nuanced light: who or what do we let define good parenting for us? Do we look to representations of strong families in the media or in our social circles as templates for our own families? We've already touched upon the reality that each family will (and should) define certain aspects of good parenting according to their individual needs and priorities; but there must also be no doubt that vitally good parenting occurs when we loosen our grips on the tailored definitions of parenting given to us by the world.

But how receptive are we to letting God play a pivotal role in defining good parenting? Only 9% of American families say that a child-nurturing faith and godliness reflects successful parenting. Maybe that statistic doesn't surprise you, but the ratio doesn't look better (24%) when we look solely at respondents who attend church regularly.[9] Most parents—churchgoers included—judge their success as parents in terms of their children's values, happiness, success, goodness, education, and self-sustaining maturity. In other words, most parents define good parenting through the imperfect and volatile lenses of good works and of the world. It is crucial that we redefine our approach to the definition of good parenting. From God's Word derives the definitive source of all truth:

> "All Scripture is inspired by God and is profitable for teaching, for rebuking, for correcting, for training in righteousness, so that the man of God may be complete, equipped for every good work" (2 Timothy 3:16-17).

24%

When the survey on the opposite page is limited to parents who attend religious services regularly, those who regard a child's faith as a mark of parenting success jumps from 9% to only 24%.

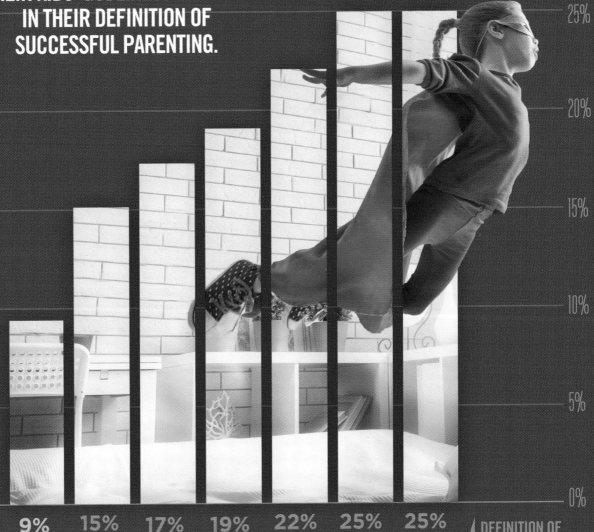

FEW AMERICAN PARENTS INCLUDE THEIR KIDS' GODLINESS OR FAITH IN THEIR DEFINITION OF SUCCESSFUL PARENTING.

25%

20%

15%

10%

5%

0%

9%
my child is godly or has faith in God

15%
my child lives independently

17%
my child graduates from college

19%
my child is a good person

22%
my child finds success in life

25%
my child becomes a happy adult

25%
my child has good values

DEFINITION OF SUCCESSFUL PARENTING

GETTING SIDETRACKED

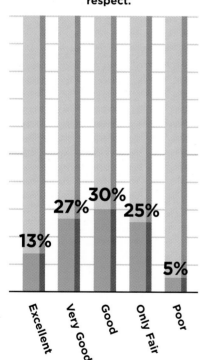

SPIRITUAL LIFE WITHIN THE FAMILY rates fairly low in American families. Only 40% of parents ranked their family's spiritual life as Very Good or Excellent. These scores were lower than categories like parental fulfillment, spending time together, and mutual respect.

13% 27% 30% 25% 5%

Excellent Very Good Good Only Fair Poor

David Platt famously pointed out that many Christians have replaced the calling of being a Christian with the magnetism of the American Dream. The American Dream, of course, can mean and signify vastly different things from person to person. Ultimately, the American Dream, with its perpetual motion of smoke and mirrors, is comprised of fragmentary little illusions and distractions—material possessions, motivators, codes of conduct—that upon closer study collapse upon their own emptiness. We may not want to admit it, but we're often quite caught up in a culture that champions the forces of consumerism and pragmatism—where we only deal in commodities and what impacts our lives today.

In this culture, we end up chasing the wrong things. No wonder so many rate their spiritual lives Only Fair or Poor. We reject the tranquility and security of a life guided by God to chase our own version of success. When this is the case, we miss out on opportunities to model positive examples to our children and make connections between life and a growing relationship with God—with the Bible as our anchor.

Our children are even more impressionable than we are to the siren song of the American Dream. One of our greatest responsibilities as parents should be regularly to take inventory of our own shortcomings and susceptibilities so that we can focus instead on the right things. This is part of our responsibility in nurturing the spiritual lives of our family.

Parents love getting their children involved with extracurricular activities. We immerse our kids in lessons and practices, encouraging them to set personal goals and to achieve their best, on a playing field or in a swimming pool, in a concert hall or in the classroom. Our kids' abilities and their talents are important, right? But are we plugging the same degree of importance in our kids' spiritual lives?

"THIS, AFTER ALL, IS THE GOAL OF THE **AMERICAN DREAM:** TO MAKE MUCH OF **OURSELVES.** BUT HERE THE GOSPEL AND THE AMERICAN DREAM ARE CLEARLY AND ULTIMATELY ANTITHETICAL TO EACH OTHER. WHILE THE GOAL OF THE AMERICAN DREAM IS **TO MAKE MUCH OF US,** THE GOAL OF THE GOSPEL IS TO **MAKE MUCH OF GOD."**

—DAVID PLATT

CHRISTIANS DON'T DEFINE THE MEANING OF LIFE ALL THAT DIFFERENTLY THAN MOST AMERICANS.

WHAT'S MY PURPOSE IN LIFE?

"Enjoying yourself is the highest goal in life."

84%
AMERICANS

66%
CHRISTIANS

"You enjoy yourself and find fulfillment in life by pursuing the things you desire most."

86%
AMERICANS

72%
CHRISTIANS

"To find yourself, look within yourself."

91%
AMERICANS

76%
CHRISTIANS

NOT THAT DIFFERENT

Is it starting to sink in that believers and nonbelievers foster very comparable philosophies concerning parenting and general success in life? Believers have an immeasurable advantage over nonbelievers in terms of their eternal salvation and understanding of God's mercy through Christ, but they are just as liable to cultural influence. Our faith does not exempt us from our human fallibility.

Consider that 91% of Americans agree with the sentiment that one can find purpose by "looking within" oneself, and 76% of Christians would echo that same sentiment. This mindset suggests that most Christians believe in placing self on the throne instead of Jesus, our Lord and Savior. Think about these other two statements. They glorify enjoyment and desire of the flesh. And the margin of difference between the general population and Christians are separated by fewer than 20%.[14] These statistics should be an alarm clock going off to us, who as Christ followers believe in denying self and taking up our cross daily.

Each of these challenges the meaning of life and are decentralized from what should be the center of a healthy Christian life: Jesus. Jesus should define our purpose. Jesus should define our way. We should take heed of the alarming lack of disparity between believers and nonbelievers in matters of purpose. As our children develop, they will be searching for deeper and deeper meanings. If we cannot remind ourselves of the truth, how then can we hope to steer our children in the right direction?

Statistics like these inform the next section. If we chase happiness by defining life as pursuing the things we desire most, then we are surely in danger of allowing someone else to develop our kids spiritually.

83% of parents
believe they should be
most responsible for
their child's spiritual
development.

But only 35%
say their religious faith is
one of the most important
influences on their
parenting.

This leaves 48%
who acknowledge their
role in their child's spiritual
development, but don't
consider their faith among
the most important
influences on their
parenting.

OUR APPROACH TO SPIRITUAL DEVELOPMENT

When American parents were asked who should be most responsible for a child's spiritual development, statistics suggest that parents do believe that they should be the principal instigators of their kids' spiritual development, but do they actually act on this freedom? Does it surprise you that 83% of parents believe that they should be the go-to household authority for questions of matters of spiritual development, but that most of these same respondents don't utilize their authority role as proactively as they should? Only 35% of parents acknowledge that their own religious faith is one of the most important influences on parenting, which leaves 48% of parents who purport to understand the importance of spiritual development but don't personally act on this need.[11]

There seems to be a disconnect somewhere within this data. More than likely, a majority of Christian parents are simply following the model of how they were discipled. Parents take on the mantle of their children's spiritual development and take their kids to church or other religious activities. Take a look at the chart on pages 36-37 to review the spiritual activities that kids do most. Church-related activities rank the highest here, while personal spiritual activities rank at the bottom. Does that sound accurate for your family?

Reflecting on this data, we begin to see a pattern. A majority of kids participate in church-related activities but only a fraction develop lasting, personal spiritual disciplines. The reality is that parents are outsourcing more of their children's spiritual development than they may recognize, even if done with the best intentions. We will discuss later that this approach is not the most effective way to instill real, lasting, and earnest Christian values in our children's lives. We can (and should) send our kids to Sunday School and Vacation Bible School, but we should not feel that this is enough. Our involvement in our kids' spiritual lives must be personal and personable.

83 PERCENT OF PARENTS AGREE THEY SHOULD BE MOST RESPONSIBLE FOR THEIR CHILD'S SPIRITUAL DEVELOPMENT.

35

62%
regularly attended Sunday School or small group

54%
attended Vacation Bible School

50%
attended youth group/youth worship as a teen

50%
participated in church social activities for children/teens

47%
regularly attended children's worship/ children's church

100%

90%

80%

70%

60%

50%

40%

30%

20%

10%

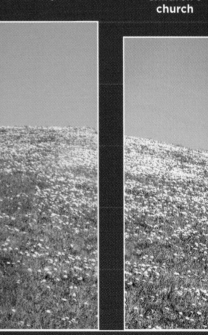

WHAT SPIRITUAL ACTIVITIES ARE KIDS DOING MOST?

CHURCH-RELATED ACTIVITIES TOP THE CHART, WHILE PERSONAL SPIRITUAL ACTIVITIES RANK AT THE BOTTOM.

44%
attended
church camps/
retreats

33%
regularly served
at church

27%
participated in
church mission
trips or projects

29%
regularly read
the Bible

28%
regularly spent
time in prayer

CHURCH ATTENDANCE IS ON THE DECLINE

"THE NUMBER OF EVANGELICAL CHURCHGOERS IS STABLE, BUT THE DEFINITION OF *'REGULAR CHURCH ATTENDANCE'* HAS CHANGED."
–TREVIN WAX

One of the starkest ironies implicit in recent studies of Christian parent behavior in the Information Age is that, even as parents increasingly outsource their children's spiritual lives, they attend church less and less. The trend shows that the number of evangelical churchgoers is stable, but their definition of regular church attendance has changed.[12] Where church members may have attended 2-3 times weekly in former generations, they attend 2-3 times monthly. Only 35% of American Christians find that "attending religious services" is an essential part of what it means to be a Christian.[13]

The world at large is a spiritual desert, and we know that the refuge of a church community is a stone's throw away ... but don't we sometimes take it for granted? Being active in a family of believers is an essential component of what it means to be a Christian—to be a healthy, thriving member of the body of Christ.

Scripture continually reinforces the role that community should play in our lives. Christ reminds us, *"For where two or three are gathered together in my name, I am there among them" (Matthew 18:20).* And the writer of Hebrews, reflecting on the need for fellow Christians to congregate, urged that we must continue to meet together: *"Not neglecting to gather together, as some are in the habit of doing, but encouraging each other, and all the more as you see the day approaching" (Hebrews 10:25).* We need Christ desperately. But we also need one another. We need to practice fellowship, and so do our children.

> **THE #1 REASON** FOR THE DECLINE IN CHURCH ATTENDANCE IS THAT MEMBERS ATTEND WITH **LESS FREQUENCY** THAN THEY DID JUST A FEW YEARS AGO.
> —THOM RAINER

SURPRISE!
WHAT DID NOT MAKE THE LIST

As parents, we know that it's our job to nurture and protect. We fasten kids in approved car seats to protect them in case of an accident. We hold their hands in parking lots and busy roads, protecting them from oncoming traffic. We bathe them daily in anti-bacterial hand sanitizer to prevent the spread of germs. We're conditioned to think that protection equals parenting.

We all have goals we would like to accomplish in our parenting. Maybe a college scholarship is number one on your list. Maybe career happiness and wealth in your child's future measures highly. Maybe it's dating, marriage, and grandkids. Maybe we just want to raise kids who follow Jesus and value holiness. Once our goals are determined, whatever they may be, the next step is deciding a route that will take us there. That's when parenting becomes tricky.

Just because a person has godly goals doesn't mean they'll fully depend on godly wisdom to lead him there. Parenting can be like a morning commute in terrible traffic. Everybody has a route they believe is faster or better—and sometimes you have to change your favorite path because of unforeseen circumstances.

Considering all the ideas we have about raising children, many of the things that we suppose will help accomplish our good goals are statistically insignificant. Many of the very good things we might rely on to help us really offer no impact on results.

In one respect, that's frightening. Discovering that family mealtimes don't earn lifelong spiritual health points can be demoralizing. Learning that all our efforts to screen media and popular culture could indeed be in vain is devastating. Understanding that some of

ACCORDING TO THE NOTHING LESS RESEARCH, MANY OF THE VERY GOOD THINGS WE (AS PARENTS) MIGHT RELY ON TO HELP US REALLY OFFER NO NOTICEABLE IMPACT ON RESULTS OF THE SPIRITUAL HEALTH OF OUR CHILDREN.

the moral hills we are prepared to die on won't lead us any closer to victory is unsettling at best, and possibly even crippling as a parent.

Read through the "Insufficient Evidence" list below and ask yourself: which ones of the responses surprise you? Which actions have deterred your focus from your final destination and gotten you lost along the way? Which ones of these have completely occupied your time and attention? Which ones surprise you that they are not on the list?

- Family **ate meals together** at least once a week
- Parent **acted differently** at church and at home
- Parents had responsibilities **serving the community**
- Parents **discussed** either everything or seldom bringing up uncomfortable topics
- Parents regularly **talked about spiritual things**
- Parents **reviewed Sunday School lessons**
- Parents **didn't hide their mistakes**
- Parents emphasized **doing the right thing**
- Parents didn't encourage child/teen to **be careful what others see them do**
- Parents encouraged the child's **personal relationship with God**
- Parents emphasized **God's grace and forgiveness**
- Family went on **vacations**, fun outings, 1-on-1 outings
- Parents **included friends** in family activities
- Parents **did not screen media** or **allow media**
- Parents **increased child responsibility** with age
- Parents **did not miss special events**
- Parents **prayed for child's relationship** with God
- Parents **prayed for God** to help child in situations they faced
- Church **size** or **consistency** at one church
- Church that family attended emphasized **the gospel**, good **behavior**, **what the Bible says**, **fun** environment, ministry **growth**, church-child **relationship building**

- The choice between **home** school, **public** school, **Christian** school, or **private** school
- Child playing **sports**, getting **good grades**, having a **job** as a teen
- Having other kids his age or **friends at church**
- Connecting with **youth pastor**
- **Sunday School** attendance, **VBS**, **youth group**, **children's worship**, social teen **activities**, **camps** and **retreats**[14]

Admittedly, many of the things on this list are very good things. Many of them should remain on our short lists of great parenting habits and family strategies. However, these actions offered insufficient evidence on the overall spiritual health of young adults. The reality is that some of the routes parents are likely to take—and recommend—may get us no closer to the destination we desire.

Parents, we want to protect our kids and also lead our kids. So what does it mean when the things we assume will help us win at both of those goals leave us empty? It means we're being offered freedom instead. Rather than guard our hearts and hands in fear, God is inviting us to recognize our limitations and trust Him. He is offering us the chance to take off the pressure to perform and eliminate all the guilt we feel over doing the wrong things and messing up the right ones. He's reminding us to focus on the best rather than getting bogged down even with good things. He's redeeming us and offering grace when we choose good things in place of His best for us.

Pressure is off. We don't have to determine the right way. And even if we do, it won't work out well. We're far better off pursuing God and trusting Him for the results.

Parenting is definitely not an exact science. We'll reference the handiwork of God as reminders that our kids are ultimately in His perfect will. The role of the Holy Spirit, no matter how often we try to step in and steal the show, will always be played by the Holy Spirit. There is accountability in that. There is freedom in that. Moving past our own

"Our greatest fear should not be of **failure** but of succeeding at things in life **that don't really matter.**"

–FRANCIS CHAN

ideas about whatever magic formulas we think will parent our kids best, we can focus on a few truths that do lead to significant impact. Then we can stop beating ourselves up, shackled in guilt by regret. Then we can rely on God to take our meager effort—and distracted focus—and multiply it for His good purpose in the life of our kids.

WE HAVE THIS HOPE

Statistics can outline opportunity, or they can overwhelm the senses. Detailed data can send us into a tailspin. We can be paralyzed in fear or wallow in regret. In those moments, we must stop and remember.

What does Scripture say about probability? What does God's Word reveal about the difficulty we face ... and even that which we, despite our best intentions, cause in life? Just as it says in Hebrews, we must remember, "We have this hope as an anchor for the soul, firm and secure" (Hebrews 6:19) and that hope is Jesus. He has gone before us in our parenting, and He will continue to guide us as we abide in Him. Don't lose hope!

There is a drastic difference between a person walking with Jesus and a person who doesn't know the eternal life found only in Christ. Even deeper, there is a dramatic distinction between nominal believers who may have at one point professed belief in Jesus and described themselves as Christians and people who daily seek God. We want to raise our kids to become sold out followers of Christ. We want to see a generation of young adults who are alive in Christ. When it comes to a person's spiritual life or, better put, spiritual aliveness, there is truly only one source of hope.

Parents and church ministry leaders, we do not function as people who have no hope. Our God can tackle our problems. Our God can focus our attention. Our God can redeem our families. Our God can transform our children into victorious spiritual champions.

WE WANT TO RAISE OUR KIDS TO BECOME SOLD OUT FOLLOWERS OF CHRIST. WE WANT TO SEE A GENERATION OF YOUNG ADULTS WHO ARE ALIVE IN CHRIST.

15 INFLUENCERS OF SPIRITUAL HEALTH

15 INFLUENCERS OF SPIRITUAL HEALTH

"NOW HE WHO PLANTS AND HE WHO WATERS ARE ONE, AND EACH WILL RECEIVE HIS OWN REWARD ACCORDING TO HIS OWN LABOR. FOR WE ARE GOD'S COWORKERS" (1 CORINTHIANS 3:8-9).

So what do we do now? With all of the studies and easy-to-read conclusions, what should parents and church leaders do to raise fully devoted Christ followers? The ultimate ability to create new growth lies with our omnipotent Gardener, but we bear the responsibility of planting and watering the seeds in the lives of our children.

As our kids grow, they should begin to tend their own soil and set their own agendas regarding spiritual disciplines. With that understanding, we must also remember God's command in Deuteronomy 11 to pass down our faith.

"Teach them to your children, talking about them when you sit in your house and when you walk along the road, when you lie down and when you get up" (Deuteronomy 11:19).

While parents trend toward outsourcing the spiritual development of children to the church, it's a job best shared. Pastors and church leadership can partner with parents to influence the lifelong spiritual health of the child. We've already seen how easy it is to become tangled up in ideals that yield no fruit. Instead, can we work together to raise our kids to become spiritual champions when they reach young adulthood? By God's grace, we believe that our combined efforts are not only preferable, but possible. Knowing the value of our collaboration, what can we do? Where do we go from here?

Question: What are the trends that stand out as influential factors? How can parents and church leaders leverage these common factors and work together to influence the spiritual health of our children?

One note: it may seem presumptive to try to measure someone spiritually. Yet we see in Peter's second letter that the evidence or confirmation of our calling should be observable. He desperately wanted us to possess these qualities in increasing measure. Our current spiritual condition questions were limited to what a parent can observe and answer objectively. We use "stronger spiritual health" throughout *Nothing Less* to describe this increased measure.

Based on the Nothing Less research, 15 characteristics are predictive of stronger spiritual health of young adults. However, they are not equal in their importance. One has the largest impact, four have moderate impact, and ten have smaller impact. Note that some actually have a negative spiritual influence.

LARGEST IMPACT
➕ Child regularly read their Bible while growing up

MODERATE IMPACT
➕ Child regularly spent time in prayer while growing up
➕ Child regularly served in church while growing up
➕ Child listened primarily to Christian music
➕ Child participated in church missions trips/projects

SMALLEST IMPACT
➖ Child did not want to go to church as a teen
➕ Child's best friend was an influence to follow Christ while growing up
➕ Child is a female
➕ Child connected with several adults at church who intentionally invested in them
➖ Child was rebellious growing up
➕ Parents typically asked forgiveness when they messed up
➕ Parents pointed out biblical principles in everyday life
➖ Child regularly listened to secular/popular music
➕ Child had siblings
➖ Family dropped in frequency of family church service attendance growing up

2,000 PROTESTANT PARENTS RANKED THE SPIRITUAL CONDITION OF THEIR YOUNG ADULT CHILDREN AND SHARED INSIGHT ABOUT THEIR CHILDHOOD. THESE ARE THE THINGS THAT MADE A DIFFERENCE.

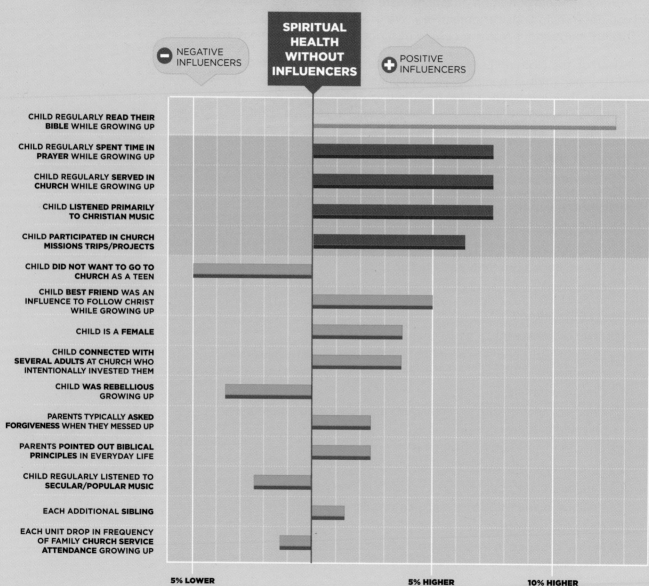

NEGATIVE INFLUENCERS

SPIRITUAL HEALTH WITHOUT INFLUENCERS

POSITIVE INFLUENCERS

CHILD REGULARLY **READ THEIR BIBLE** WHILE GROWING UP

CHILD REGULARLY **SPENT TIME IN PRAYER** WHILE GROWING UP

CHILD REGULARLY **SERVED IN CHURCH** WHILE GROWING UP

CHILD **LISTENED PRIMARILY TO CHRISTIAN MUSIC**

CHILD PARTICIPATED IN CHURCH **MISSIONS TRIPS/PROJECTS**

CHILD **DID NOT WANT TO GO TO CHURCH** AS A TEEN

CHILD **BEST FRIEND** WAS AN INFLUENCE TO FOLLOW CHRIST WHILE GROWING UP

CHILD IS A **FEMALE**

CHILD **CONNECTED WITH SEVERAL ADULTS** AT CHURCH WHO INTENTIONALLY INVESTED THEM

CHILD **WAS REBELLIOUS** GROWING UP

PARENTS TYPICALLY **ASKED FORGIVENESS** WHEN THEY MESSED UP

PARENTS **POINTED OUT BIBLICAL PRINCIPLES** IN EVERYDAY LIFE

CHILD REGULARLY LISTENED TO **SECULAR/POPULAR MUSIC**

EACH ADDITIONAL **SIBLING**

EACH UNIT DROP IN FREQUENCY OF FAMILY **CHURCH SERVICE ATTENDANCE** GROWING UP

5% LOWER THAN THE SPIRITUAL LEVEL

5% HIGHER THAN THE SPIRITUAL LEVEL

10% HIGHER THAN THE SPIRITUAL LEVEL

NOTE: IMPACTS WHILE CONTROLLING FOR OTHER INFLUENCERS. INFLUENCERS CAN BE COMBINED.

Since some of these characteristics address the same topic and demographics the child cannot change, we will take these helpful statistics and group them into 10 categories.

Among the factors on this list, there are nearly unlimited blends of influence, and the influence is cumulative. Consider all the types of cake you've tried. Ratios and flavors can vary greatly, but basic ingredients are about the same: flour, sugar, eggs, etc. Just as those basic ingredients are building blocks to make any type of cake, these 10 spiritual building blocks provide a solid foundation for intentional parenting and creating a purpose-filled partnership between church and home.

That said, there is no perfect recipe. There are no solid guarantees. We have all met the parents who seemingly did everything right. We have all met the moms and dads employing each of the spiritual influencers outlined in this section to nearly perfect degrees whose children stray from faith as young adults. The sinful human condition may prevail despite our best efforts, but obedience to God's call, faith in Christ's power, and reliance on the Spirit's guidance won't allow us to give up.

Ultimately, the nature, personality, and temperament of a child must be considered along with the divine will of our Father. First, trust fully that God will grant wisdom to those of us who seek it.

"Now if any of you lacks wisdom, he should ask God — who gives to all generously and ungrudgingly — and it will be given to him" (James 1:5).

Next, press into each of the following carefully defined influencers to shape the overall spiritual health of your child. Each child will be different. Each family will operate differently. Each church will provide unique levels of leadership and support. Forced compliance will likely lead to more rebellion than avid participation. So, parenting must blend proactive encouragement and patience. Passing faith is paramount. Helping our kids mature into young adults who know and follow Jesus is the aim. Applying these 10 spiritual influencers in your family can help.

10 Categories of Spiritual Influencers

1. Bible Reading
2. Prayer
3. Serving
4. Music
5. Mission Trips or Projects
6. Interest Level in Church
7. Influence by Others
8. Influence by Parents
9. Gender & Siblings
10. Church Attendance

1

A child who read his Bible regularly while growing up has 12.5% stronger spiritual health as a young adult.[15]

THE NUMBER ONE SPIRITUAL INDICATOR — BIBLE READING

Affirming our belief in the supremacy of God's Word, the single greatest influence over spiritual health is regular Bible reading while growing up. Plainly put, the parents of young adults indicate that regular Bible reading as children yield the greatest influence over their spiritual health.

We should have known that, right? It's the simple Sunday School answer. Bible!

The single greatest contribution to raising fully-devoted, Christ-following young adults is regular — not daily or religiously, just regular — Bible reading. This lone factor forms the first tier of statistically significant predictors. Rightfully so! Scripture makes it clear.

It's an easy assertion for believers to make that the Bible is our source for God's revelation to all people. It's a common confession for Christ-followers to express that the Bible is a source for daily living. But do we just as readily make the leap to admit the lifelong effect that reading the Bible throughout childhood yields later in life? The writer of Proverbs did: *"Start a youth out on his way; even when he grows old he will not depart from it" (Proverbs 22:6).*

There is something special about the word "way" in this verse. It's the same Hebrew word used in Psalm 25 to reference both God's way and the way to raise the child as God designed. The wisdom writer isn't talking about teaching kids simple choices between right and wrong. He's addressing the connection between a kid who is pointed to the truth and an adult who remains faithful to it. This proverb is a promise from God, who always keeps His promises. In fact, all the promises He made—no matter how numerous—find their

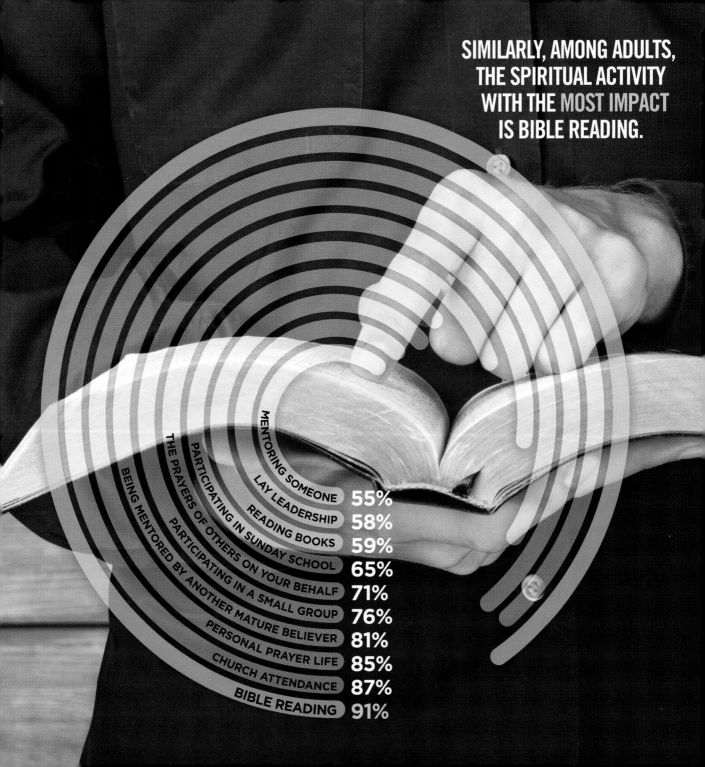

SIMILARLY, AMONG ADULTS, THE SPIRITUAL ACTIVITY WITH THE MOST IMPACT IS BIBLE READING.

MENTORING SOMEONE 55%
LAY LEADERSHIP 58%
READING BOOKS 59%
PARTICIPATING IN SUNDAY SCHOOL 65%
THE PRAYERS OF OTHERS ON YOUR BEHALF 71%
PARTICIPATING IN A SMALL GROUP 76%
BEING MENTORED BY ANOTHER MATURE BELIEVER 81%
PERSONAL PRAYER LIFE 85%
CHURCH ATTENDANCE 87%
BIBLE READING 91%

89%

**Percentatge
of households
that own a Bible**

4.1

**Average number
of Bibles per
household**

19%

**Percentage of
Protestant churchgoers
who read the Bible daily.**

fulfillment in Jesus. Paul reminds early believers (and us) of that fact, *"For every one of God's promises is 'Yes' in him" (2 Corinthians 1:20).*

The Bible points us to Jesus, the only true Way, so this first influencer makes perfect sense. Regular Bible reading makes the greatest difference in a child's long term spiritual health.

BUT WE HAVE A PROBLEM

We should all be breathing deep sighs of relief. Aren't you glad, as a parent or church leader, that an advanced degree in systematic theology isn't required to raise spiritual giants? If an essential key to raising kids into young adults, who are not only professing Christians but growing parts of a local church body, is simply regular Bible reading, what on earth could the problem be? All we need to do is dust off our Scripture and develop a plan. Can it really be just that simple?

Well, let's start by asking serial dieters. Regarding the physical body, we know that diet and exercise are the clear-cut answers to maintaining a healthy weight. We also know that eating right and exercising regularly are easier said than done. Maybe the same is true of this important discipline.

Then consider for a moment your mother's wedding china. How many times can you remember eating from those dishes? Owning something is quite different from using it. Alas, this isn't research on material possessions we own but never use or no longer need. That's a different publication all together. This research reveals that the Bible is America's most beloved book. As high as 89% of all American households own a copy, but only one in five churchgoers reads the Bible every day. Meanwhile, 23% of Americans have read a few sentences or less from the Bible — ever.

53 PERCENT OF AMERICANS HAVE READ
ONLY SEVERAL BIBLE PASSAGES OR LESS.

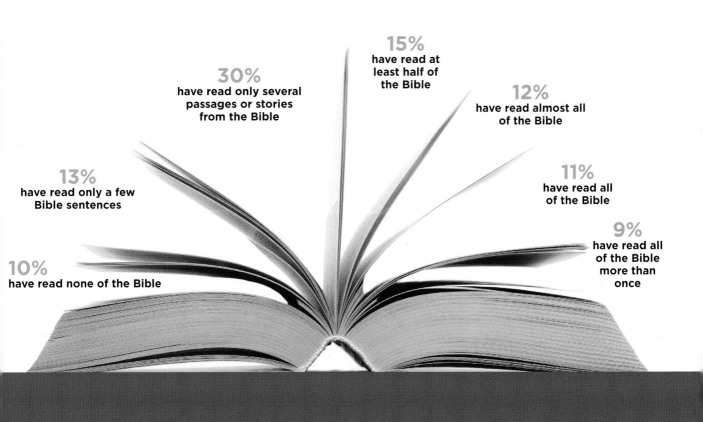

15%
have read at
least half of
the Bible

12%
have read almost all
of the Bible

30%
have read only several
passages or stories
from the Bible

13%
have read only a few
Bible sentences

11%
have read all
of the Bible

10%
have read none of the Bible

9%
have read all
of the Bible
more than
once

"Here in the US, the problem isn't that people don't own a Bible. It's that they don't read the Bible they have,"[16] notes Eric Geiger, Vice President of LifeWay Resources.

Why not? Hectic lives likely top the list of excuses. However, that obvious response might be a smoke screen for a larger issue. Perhaps it comes down to comprehension; owning a Bible does not equate to understanding it. The root of this issue could be as simple as struggling with a translation or as complex as lack of discipleship. To some extent, ignoring the value of reading God's Word regularly could also be synonymous with the fast-food culture: despite our desire for immediate results, Scripture-reading is more often a long-term investment.

One thing is clear: reading God's Word regularly throughout childhood yields undeniable results. So regardless of the reasons Bibles collect dust on shelves, we must determine a way to prioritize usage to raise growing Christ-followers.

> "THE BIBLE IS THE VOICE OF GOD IN PRINT."
> –TONY EVANS

WHAT CAN THE CHURCH DO?

We can't argue the existence of the problem. Piling on pressure, guilt, and shame are neither godly nor good responses. So what can church leaders do to aid families?

First and foremost, church leaders must know their role and own it. We've all likely heard this common expression regarding the process of leaving or rethinking church attendance: "I just wasn't being fed." When is the last time you heard a grown-up in a fancy restaurant complain in the same manner? The chef may have been charged with preparing the meal and the wait staff with serving it, but the customer has to pick up his own fork to be fed. The church must begin with a solid discipleship model empowering moms and dads to grow in Christ and take responsibility for their spiritual maturity. That, of course, includes an emphasis on regular Bible reading.

"Here in the U.S., **the problem** isn't that people **don't own a Bible.** It's that they don't read **the Bible they have.**"

–ERIC GEIGER

EVERY CHILD
SHOULD HAVE
ACCESS TO A
VERSION OF
THE BIBLE THEY
CAN READ AND
UNDERSTAND,
ONE THAT
DOESN'T WATER
DOWN OR
COMPROMISE
TRUTH.

Is it enough to raise the banner of the Bible and continually teach the value of Scripture reading? Does equipping parents with solid food and self-feeding skills automatically translate at home? Not when parents default to hoping the church will handle all of the disciple-making skills.

First, every child should have access to a version of the Bible they can read and understand, one that doesn't water down or compromise truth but is written at an appropriate reading and developmental level.

Other important ideas include regular use of Scripture in teaching and ministry programming. Games, songs, skits, and media are all great supplements. The key word is *supplements*. The primary tool should always be Scripture. Even when using a curriculum guide or paraphrased story, a leader should hold the Bible and pause to share how important it is to read directly from God's Word.

Beyond providing adequate help choosing Bibles and raising the banner of regular Bible reading, are there other ways to support the habit of regular Bible reading for kids? Like our overall approach to spiritual health, it's not an exact science, but here are other ideas to incorporate:

- **Provide Bible reading plans** or accompaniment pieces like daily devotionals.
- **Offer resources** like Bible dictionaries, concordances, and commentaries.
- **Help kids understand** the different testaments and types of literature in the Bible.
- **Help kids learn** fun, wild, and interesting stories and facts that might be unfamiliar.
- **Always be willing to share** how the Bible helps you personally in everyday life.

WHAT TOOLS CAN HELP?

Sounding the alarm for biblical literacy and commitment is an ongoing challenge that must remain present among church leadership. Pastors, in particular, bear the responsibility of not only expositing truth but being a constant reminder of how immersing ourselves in the truth is the call of every disciple.

Beyond championing the importance of personal Bible reading for parents and family, church leaders are taking an important step. Supporting what we hope is happening at home with solid, biblically-based programs at church is a great way to bring church and home together to further spiritual growth.

Solid, biblically-based programs accomplish the following:

1 **Pointing kids to the beauty of God's Word** in your regular ministry programming times whets their appetites for even more biblical learning at home.

2 **Providing resources to help parents** continue the learning at home supports their call as the primary disciple-makers of their children and combats the default attitude of some parents to outsource all aspects of faith development to the church.

3 **Solid, biblically-based programs** specific to the development of each phase of childhood ensure that the concepts communicated can actually be understood and acquired by kids.

4 **Finally, focusing on Scripture** allows the Holy Spirit to do what only He can do—draw kids to Christ in faith. The Bible is the force that makes ministry transformational, rather than merely educational.

LEVELS OF BIBLICAL LEARNING®

HOW CAN I LEARN MORE ABOUT LEVELS OF BIBLICAL LEARNING?

Visit *www.lifeway.com/ levelsofbiblicallearning* for free downloads and training.

LifeWay offers resources to help in every stage of childhood development. Because resources follow the Levels of Biblical Learning, you can trust that each ministry plan and curriculum offering is both developmentally appropriate and theologically sound.

What exactly is the Levels of Biblical Learning (LOBL)? LOBL is a map of biblical truths organized into ten key categories. The categories compose the theological and doctrinal truths children need to form a biblical worldview and know the God of the Bible. The ten categories are God, Jesus, Holy Spirit, Bible, Salvation, Creation, Church, People, Family, Community & World. Each of these categories introduces the appropriate truth at just the right developmental age.

BIBLE SKILLS FOR KIDS

In a similar way, Bible Skills for Kids provides milestone Bible skills along the way to ensure that children are grasping key concepts and exhibiting key abilities to navigate the Bible at each stage of development.

HOW CAN I LEARN MORE ABOUT BIBLE SKILLS FOR KIDS?

Visit *www.lifeway.com/ bibleskillsforkids* for free downloads and training.

Whether you follow curriculum plans from **Bible Studies for Life**, **Explore the Bible, The Gospel Project**, **TeamKID**, or any LifeWay Kids product line, you can be certain that LOBL and Bible Skills for Kids have guided its development, ensuring that biblical truth remains at the forefront.

We know and believe that Paul's words to Timothy regarding Scripture are true:

"All Scripture is inspired by God and is profitable for teaching, for rebuking, for correcting, for training in righteousness, so that the

"The more time we spend in God's Word, the more we become like Him.

Imagine what would happen in our churches, in our nation, and in our world if all believers were experiencing the transforming power of God's Word on a daily basis."

–THOM RAINER

man of God may be complete, equipped for every good work" (2 Timothy 3:16-17).

What does good curriculum for ministry programming do? It takes the Word of God and follows a clear path so that even kids can be taught, steered, corrected, and trained. It starts them out early on the road toward completion and readiness for the good works God has prepared for them. It keeps the Bible high on display so that one day, looking back, our kids will have grown into young adults who recall regularly reading the Bible during childhood. They'll look back and remember that the Bible was a key feature at church and at home and remember the great lessons they learned as they grew. They'll quip, "How could I consider growing up and departing from such a good Word? I need it too much. It's simply part of who I am."

That is the vision and prayer. Young adults who know God's Word and do God's Word because they heard it and loved it as children.

WHAT CAN THE FAMILY DO?

In a July 2017 LifeWay *Facts & Trends* article, Dr. Thom Rainer writes, "The more time we spend in God's Word, the more we become like Him. Imagine what would happen in our churches, in our nation, and in our world if all believers were experiencing the transforming power of God's Word on a daily basis."[29]

Add homes to the mix, and imagine what would happen in children's lives if they saw the value of Scripture for everyday living modeled for them on a daily basis. Imagine the impact on their futures if regular Bible reading at their level became part of their consistent routines.

Let's get practical. What can families actually do to instill the value of regular Bible reading and devotional living?

29%
of kids regularly read the Bible when they were growing up. (Nothing Less Study)

HOW HAS BIBLE READING WORKED FOR YOUR FAMILY?

"

I kind of view getting the kids into reading through their Bibles like getting kids to sit in 'big church' with their parents: they may not be understanding everything but it is good for them to get exposure to it, and some things will stick. Being a family of "check-listers" we create a Bible reading chart for each kid. Some hit more than others in terms of consistency, but we do 'assign' it and they get more than if we didn't.

–Unchong, Mom of 3, Illinois

"

My husband offered $100 a year to any kid to read through the Bible with any version or plan. One made it and got $100 at Christmas when he was 11. He was the only one that went for it. Sadly, we got a lot of "Meh" from the others. My husband and I took the approach to have our Quiet Times out in the open and hoped the "caught not taught" ions would seep into their DNA.

–Lisa, Mom of 5, Indiana

JASON loves reading his Bible that has sports devotionals incorporated, where athletes tell about their favorite Scriptures and testimonies of being Christians on the field.

PRISCILLA SHIRER SPEAKS SCRIPTURE: I am very intentional about speaking affirmative scripturally-based statements over my boys. Most of the time, as soon as I start in on the liturgy of "You are …" statements, they frantically lift their hands up over their ears as if to say, "Mom, enough already, we hear this every day!"

JONATHAN and **CHRISTOPHER** participated in Bible Drill throughout childhood, memorizing dozens of Scriptures.

JANA MAGRUDER INTERVIEWED DAVID PLATT:

"David shared that family devotional and Bible reading at the Platt house often was a mix of reading and praying together, but quickly turned into wrestling and playing!"

"We always knew family Bible time would be a part of our kids' upbringing, but the reality is, we've struggled to make it work. Our younger child has always been open to the gospel and loves our Bible-reading time together, but our older child has always resisted. The more we try to gently encourage or even push, the more resistance we get. When you have a child who simply won't do it, it's pretty discouraging. We are just praying for God to change her heart.

–Michael, Dad of 2, New York

"We've tried to go after the Bible as life rather than an event. To this end, we will share what we are reading/learning at dinner and talk about it with the boys. When they were little, we loved all the storybook resources that helped them get a foundation that the Bible isn't a bunch of loosely strung together morality stories to help them be good. One summer all the kids got a reading plan from our church. It was great ... for the summer. Everything kind of goes downhill when school starts! We've had grand plans for family Bible time, but they never last more than a week!

–Robin, Mom of 2, Michigan

As little kids, storybook and first reader Bibles were a big win. We used to read a passage with the kids before school bus pickup and then pray, but that sometimes turned into a 5-minute rushed thing. Recently, my oldest son has been inspired to read his Bible regularly after going to a youth conference, but the other two roll their eyes every time I mention Bible reading.

–Judy, Mom of 3, Pennsylvania

TYSON and **TATE'S** parents write Scripture passages on a large chalkboard in their kitchen. They read and memorize throughout the week.

PROVIDE A MODEL FOR BIBLE READING.

First, moms and dads can model a lifestyle of faithful Bible reading (and we will see Bible reading and family devotions again in Chapter 4).

At some point in their lives, your children might have lived under the assumption that you were a superhero who could do no wrong. Whether the light bulb moment of parent fallibility has occurred in your house yet or not, it will. As parents, we know that what we model has a far greater impact than what we instruct or enforce. Parents should never attempt to model perfection or to portray an unrealistic, unattainable standard to their children. The goal is first consistency, then authenticity. Our ultimate goal should be to display and live out the gospel by seeking Christ in all we do but asking forgiveness when we fall short.

When studying parent behavior, statistically significant predictors of spiritual health meld together like a recipe. Lower on the list, but still registering as indicators, are two positive influencers regarding parents:

1. **Parents typically pointed out biblical principles** in everyday life as kids were growing up.

2. **Parents typically asked forgiveness** when they messed up as kids were growing up.

Two obvious connections shout loudly in these two statements. First, a parent can't point out biblical principles without reading the Bible, at least not accurately or authentically. As parents engage Scripture and become more like Jesus, they mature their ability to see the world through a biblical lens and gain a Holy Spirit-driven opportunity to point out the truths they learn to their kids along the way. Second, we can't underestimate the power of forgiveness. Scripture links the idea of forgiveness to another faith essential.

"LEADING A FAMILY STARTS WITH BEING IN A VITAL AND FLOURISHING RELATIONSHIP WITH GOD THROUGH JESUS CHRIST. JESUS' OWN LEADERSHIP FLOWED FROM HIS INTIMACY WITH THE FATHER."
–ERIC MASON

As disciplined as we strive to be regarding God's Word, there will undoubtedly be moments when we fail to live it out. Enter confession, followed by forgiveness and an opportunity for parents to incorporate this key spiritual health predictor. This one will surface again later, most likely because opportunities to make confession and seek forgiveness certainly aren't limited to failure to consistently read the Bible and live it out.

Next, moms and dads can carve out time and create priorities for their kids to engage in regular Bible reading too.

When your children were infants, it was likely a battle to set the feeding and sleeping schedule. Your daily routine was governed, at least to some degree, by the needs of a tiny human. Over time, however, you gained control. As your children grew, you determined bed times, meal times, and even menus. Parents set their priorities. Spiritually, that matters too.

In the home, kids need to see their moms and dads deep in the Word of God. They also need time carved out and regularly set aside for them to do the same. When they are non-readers or early readers, this is obviously a parent-child activity. As children grow, moms and dads should establish a spiritual rhythm where family devotion or Bible reading is a regular part of each child's individual habits, creating disciplines as consistent as brushing their teeth.

There is a growing pressure for the outside world to determine a parent's priorities, and a very real epidemic in which children become a parent's top priority, thereby setting all other family values and priorities by their desires. Ultimately, that's a trap in which the enemy would love to ensnare us. God, in His wisdom, set parents over children. Families can ensure that children grow up with a history of regular Bible reading by setting the priority early, carving out time, and making it a consistent family practice.

Imagine the impact if moms and dads not only model this discipline, but prioritize it and work hard to protect it.

"THEREFORE, CONFESS YOUR SINS TO ONE ANOTHER AND PRAY FOR ONE ANOTHER, SO THAT YOU MAY BE HEALED" (JAMES 5:16).

WHEN INTERVIEWED ABOUT BIBLE READERSHIP, MOMS SAID ... KIDS WHO CAN'T UNDERSTAND OR RELATE TO THEIR BIBLE SHUT DOWN AND STOP READING.

MOMS SAY.

IF KIDS CAN'T RELATE TO OR DON'T UNDER-STAND THEIR BIBLE ...

They shut down.

They quit.

They give up.

They grow resentful.

MOMS SAY.

IF KIDS UNDERSTAND THEIR BIBLE ...

"It's awesome."

They can apply it.

They want to learn more.

They continue to learn on their own.

They get excited.

CHOOSE AN APPROPRIATE BIBLE FOR YOUR CHILD.

Selecting an appropriate Bible is an important part of making Bible reading both accessible and desirable for kids. For regular Bible reading to be a reality in the life of your children, they must have a Bible they want to read and can understand.

Choosing a Bible isn't rocket science, and you don't need an advanced theological degree to make a wise selection. That's especially true when you are aware that whatever Bible you choose for your 8 year old will likely not be the best by the time he hits eighth grade. Here are a couple ideas and guidelines to aid the process of choosing the appropriate Bible for your child at this particular stage:

1. **Choose a version that is user-friendly.** Make sure whatever Bible you select has all the appropriate helps, such as a table of contents and topical index. Tabs and page numbers make it easy to locate books, passages, and verses. Study helps and devotional topics are additional bonuses.

2. **Choose the translation that best fits your child's current reading level and still allows room for growth.** The goal is an accurate but accessible translation. Also consider size and durability. The Bible you choose should be easily held and managed with a binding that can stand up against what will hopefully be tons of use. At the end of the day, choosing a Bible for your child isn't as important as using the Bible with your child.

USE A BIBLE READING PLAN.

Just how was that greatest influencer of spiritual health worded on the original survey? "Child read the Bible regularly while growing up."

We've hinted at the importance of regularity in Bible reading, and we believe the best way to achieve this goal is by making and following a plan. Consider the importance of scheduling and routine in other areas of child's life. You already know the value of consistent bedtime regimens, nap time, mealtimes, and daily schedules. You likely already have plans in place for completing homework and household chores.

When it comes to regularly engaging Scripture, having a plan to follow is really half the battle. For adults, the most natural time to begin a new plan is the start of the New Year. For many families, the start of a new school year presents a similar opportunity.

Consider these ideas when selecting a Bible reading plan specifically for kids.

1. **Continuity counts.** Does your current ministry curriculum plan offer at-home devotional readings that supplement the Bible story and Bible truth from your weekend program? If so, plan weekly Bible readings to accompany your ongoing kids ministry Bible study plan.

2. **Bitesize bits.** Remember the last time you attempted to read the entire Bible in a year? It most likely required you to consume passages from both Old and New Testaments daily, sometimes several lengthy chapters from each. We want to create early wins to build ongoing success. Sticking to succinct passages that kids can read in 10-15 minutes to create a consistent habit matters more than checking off every single verse from every single book in a calendar year. Recently we interviewed Robby Gallaty about the heart behind his Bible-reading plan, *Foundations for Kids*. He said, in summary, that he and his wife created a reading plan that allowed kids and families to read their Bibles daily with a plan that takes them through the grand narrative of Scripture in a year. The goal being to help kids not lose steam by the time they reach Leviticus.

3 **Prioritize comprehension.** Open your Bible to both Leviticus 17 and 1 Samuel 17. One is clearly more difficult to understand and apply than the other. While the whole counsel of God's Word is valuable, and kids should be exposed to all of it, the priority of a reading plan for kids is creating opportunities to understand the basics of our faith. Plan readings from passages that kids can know and understand.

Use a plan kids can check off to monitor progress along the way. Consider the value of family time when each person utilizes the same plan. Dialogue transforms private disciplines into accountable actions. That matters in discipleship. Remember to start out as you intend to go and stick with it. If and when you miss, pick back up and keep going.

COMMIT TO JUST DO IT.

Back to the most obvious connection point. Topping the list in its own top tier of spiritual health predictors is regular Bible reading. Combine that with parents pointing out biblical principles in everyday life, and you have a successful recipe. Both of these conditions require a common denominator that is simply stated but challenging to practice: parental commitment.

Before any of us dive into another spiritual commitment, we must remind ourselves of some "parenting permissions."

First, parents have permission to say no. We can say no to an additional extracurricular activity. We can say no to one more regularly scheduled evening out. We can say no even to good things to allow time for the best.

Next, parents have permission to parent our kids differently. We don't have to keep up with the Joneses or even our own parents.

HOW CAN I LEARN MORE ABOUT FOUNDATIONS FOR KIDS?

Visit *www.lifeway.com/foundations* to learn more about this reading plan through God's Word.

AMONG CHURCHGOERS,
90% AGREE
WITH THE STATEMENT
**"I DESIRE TO
PLEASE AND
HONOR JESUS**
IN ALL THAT I DO."

Comparison leads to depression. We have permission to be different and parent differently.

Finally, we have permission to fail. We don't have to be perfect. We have permission to try something new and evaluate things that work and don't. We have permission to tweak along the way. Failure can work in our favor because it provides the ever important opportunity to admit it when we miss the mark and ask for forgiveness. Reminder: parents who are willing to ask forgiveness also ranked as a top influencer of spiritual health.

Enjoying those permissions and walking tall in light of God's grace, we must now turn toward commitment. What can parents do?

Parents can be specific. What exactly is the commitment you are making to engage Scripture as a family and carve out time for kids to read the Bible? Be clear from the beginning. God doesn't author confusion, but the enemy sure does, and people are often far too helpful when it comes to Satan's schemes. Do yourself a favor by being simple and to the point. You and your kids will be glad you did.

Parents can also be strategic. Jesus didn't send the disciples out to do things He hadn't first demonstrated. When it comes to Bible reading, parents should provide a model and mentor kids to copy their commitment. That's a clear-cut discipleship strategy that worked for Jesus. Why would we want to try it any other way? When we commit to regular Bible reading, we commit both to the Lord and to the precious kids He has entrusted to us.

How do those with evangelical beliefs typically approach reading the Bible on their own?

 49% I systematically read through a section a little each day.

 46% I look up verses or sections suggested by others.

 45% I look up things when I have a need.

 36% I look up things when I want to help someone else.

 31% I reread favorite stories or meaningful sections.

 27% I flip it open and read where my eyes land.

 13% I read a big chunk at one time.

 3% I do not read the Bible on my own.

WHY AREN'T WE READING?

Only 19% of believers read the Bible daily.

Let's be frank. What is really holding us back? If we as parents and church ministry leaders truly know and believe that God's Word is transformative and essential for everyday living, why aren't we reading it?

The Bible is a powerful influence. The more we read it, the more apt we are to obey God. The more we read the Bible, the more ready we are to serve Him and others and to share our faith in Jesus. The more we read God's Word, the more eagerly we seek God, build healthy relationships, and live out faith in everyday life.[18]

There are numerous reasons why believers walk blindly without His Word. Consider your own seasons of failing to read. Perhaps you have a strong connection to regular Bible reading now, but evaluate dry spells you've walked through along the way. What were your reasons then?

In the bar graph on the next page are some common reasons Americans say they don't read the Bible. You may or not relate to them, but you can likely see their creep in among Christ followers today.

We all have our reasons for neglecting God's Word. Ultimately, the power of the Holy Spirit drawing us and changing us from within is all the impetus needed to create a desire for truth in us that can only be satisfied by Scripture. It's not just a book to read, but a relationship to develop by listening to His Word. Pray that God will move in you and free you from anything holding you back.

In a survey of 2,930 Protestant churchgoers, more than half read the Bible only once a week or less.

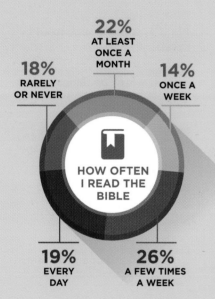

22%
AT LEAST ONCE A MONTH

18%
RARELY OR NEVER

14%
ONCE A WEEK

HOW OFTEN I READ THE BIBLE

19%
EVERY DAY

26%
A FEW TIMES A WEEK

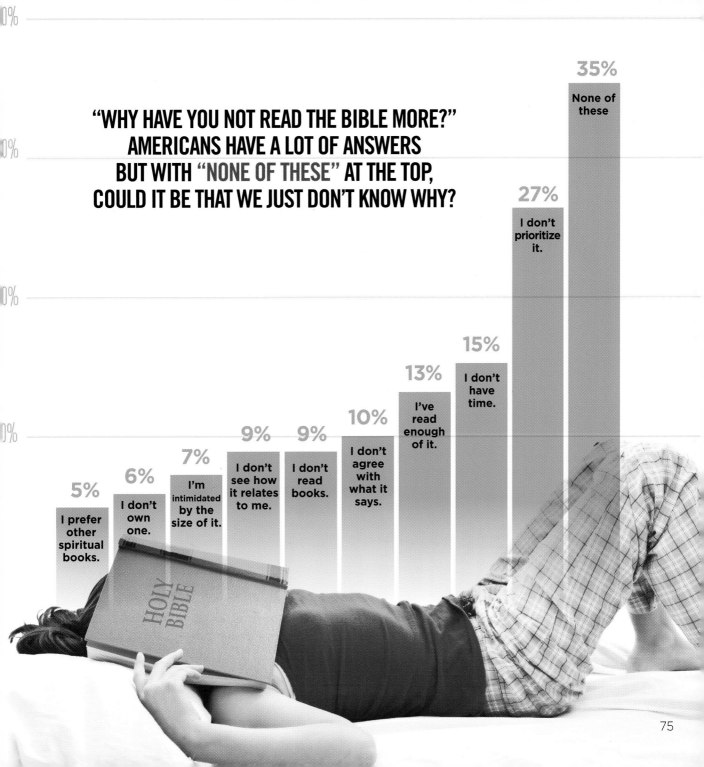

"WHY HAVE YOU NOT READ THE BIBLE MORE?"
AMERICANS HAVE A LOT OF ANSWERS
BUT WITH "NONE OF THESE" AT THE TOP,
COULD IT BE THAT WE JUST DON'T KNOW WHY?

5% — I prefer other spiritual books.

6% — I don't own one.

7% — I'm intimidated by the size of it.

9% — I don't see how it relates to me.

9% — I don't read books.

10% — I don't agree with what it says.

13% — I've read enough of it.

15% — I don't have time.

27% — I don't prioritize it.

35% — None of these

2

A child who regularly spent time in prayer while growing up has 7.5% stronger spiritual health as a young adult.[19]

PRAYER

The indicators with moderate impact on spiritual health start strong. A child who regularly spent time praying while growing up has 7.5 percent stronger spiritual health as a young adult.

Prayer is an important spiritual practice even among the general population. More than half of churchgoing Protestant parents say that they prayed as a family at least once a week, with the majority of those praying several times per week. Only 25% of those parents say they either never or rarely prayed together as a family. That should be a very encouraging statistic for pastors and church leaders today.

Consider briefly how you typically open and close your prayers. The opening declaration "Dear Father" is a common one. Ponder for just a moment the invitation we've been given to confidently call the great God of this vast universe Our Father.

"Therefore, you should pray like this: Our Father in heaven, your name be honored as holy" (Matthew 6:9).

In closing prayers, there seems to be a tendency among Protestants and Evangelicals to say, "In your name" or "In Jesus' name." That final phrase before the closing "Amen" indicates an important distinction. While the religiously polytheistic among us may believe in the power of prayer or spirituality, Christ followers are praying to a living God through the invitation of His Son.

Perhaps making this type of Father/Son prayer part of your family routine offers children a theological foundation that will carry them into adulthood. We all must readily admit our need for God the Father. He alone is our Need-Meeter, Wisdom-Provider, Caregiver, Problem-Solver, and Life-Giver. Regular prayer orients a family

52% OF CHURCHGOING PARENTS SAY THEIR FAMILY HAS FAMILY PRAYER AT LEAST ONCE A WEEK.

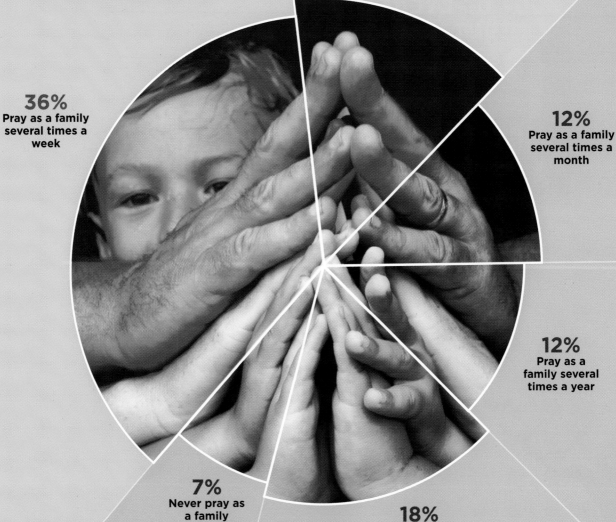

16%
Pray as a family weekly

12%
Pray as a family several times a month

36%
Pray as a family several times a week

12%
Pray as a family several times a year

7%
Never pray as a family

18%
Rarely pray as a family

toward God and continually reminds us who we are as people who desperately need Him.

We must also readily admit our need for a Savior. Jesus is the only reason we are able to stand forgiven before God, commune in relationship with a holy God, and express our needs to this great God. Prayer doesn't just proclaim who God is and explain how we come to Him, it continually reveals who we are. Our great need for God's power, presence, and purpose is what we as parents and church leaders long to have stick in kids' lives as they grow.

Prayer is certainly communion with God. We ought to teach our kids the value of both speaking to God and listening to Him. Children must be taught to pray, much like Eli taught Samuel to listen to the voice of God (1 Samuel 3). Note that this personal aspect of these indicators is beginning to surface. There is a reason that "kids regularly spent time in prayer" rose to the top of the list rather than "parents prayed for me." Kids spending time in prayer is life-changing.

28%
of kids regularly
spent time in prayer
as a child.
(Nothing Less Study)

We also ought to work to help children understand proper parts of prayer outside of our most obvious need of supplication. Prayer in our families should be times of thanksgiving, praise, confession, and also memory verse meditation. Prayer is a theological exercise and can be used in a powerful way to plant good theology into their hearts and minds. As we pray, we must pray with the gospel in mind. We should include the names, attributes, and commands of God. We not only should choose to include our requests, but also utter statements of submission to God no matter His answer. Prayer is a chance to tell Him that we will love and trust Him regardless of outcome.

Regular prayer in families is a chance to model the importance of this spiritual discipline, but it's also a way to teach our children to think and act theologically in life.[20]

3

A child who regularly served in church while growing up has 7.5% stronger spiritual health as a young adult.[21]

SERVING

"And he himself gave some to be apostles, some prophets, some evangelists, some pastors and teachers, equipping the saints for the work of ministry, to build up the body of Christ, until we all reach unity in the faith and in the knowledge of God's Son, growing into maturity with a stature measured by Christ's fullness"
(Ephesians 4:11-13).

Too many times in this passage we isolate verses 11 and 12, stopping with the building up of the body of Christ. Enter verse thirteen. The key characteristic of each person within that unified body was spiritual maturity and Christlikeness.

Paul was right about serving. It's an essential part of discipleship. As soon as a believer graduates from equating spiritual growth as being led and fed into a more accurate definition of following Jesus, service starts to count. That believer begins to understand his responsibility in the body as not only Christian duty, but also an essential component in his own spiritual growth.

With an equally high effect as prayer, serving is also included among the indicators having moderate impact on spiritual health. A child who regularly served in church while growing up has 7.5 percent stronger spiritual health as a young adult. This coincides with a 2007 study comparing young adults who stayed in the church with those who dropped out. It revealed this trend: 16% more of those who stayed had regular responsibilities within the church.[22]

Parents and church leaders, we have an incredible challenge before us. This is the epitome of leading with the end in mind. Having kids serve, lead, and take responsibility may not be the quickest way to prop up our commitment to excellence. It may also take extra time and people to make sure that kids and teens are safe. It is important to abide by safety rules that take into account that a child cannot

IN 2007 RESEARCH THAT COMPARED YOUNG ADULTS WHO STAYED IN THE CHURCH WITH THOSE WHO DROPPED OUT, 16% MORE OF THOSE WHO STAYED IN CHURCH HAD REGULAR RESPONSIBILITIES AT THE CHURCH.

be alone with one adult. Nor should a child or teen be alone with a group of kids. But choosing only called, experienced, maturing adults to bear the entire burden of God's work within the local church bypasses some incredible passages of Scripture. Not only that, leaving service to the spiritually mature is incredibly detrimental to the long-term health of the church as a whole and that of each believer within it.

> Paul wrote these words to his young protege, Timothy: "Don't let anyone despise your youth, but set an example for the believers in speech, in conduct, in love, in faith, and in purity" (1 Timothy 4:12).

Not only can young people learn to serve, but they can do it in a way that is safe and serves as an example to all believers, including those older and more mature. Paul also gave instructions to Titus regarding young people:

> "In the same way, encourage the young men to be self-controlled in everything. Make yourself an example of good works with integrity and dignity in your teaching" (Titus 2:6-7).

What if children who have opportunities to serve become teenagers who have opportunities to lead, who grow into young adults who live remarkable lives of faith without wavering in their commitment to the local church?

Finding ways to foster service and allow ministry opportunities for children requires extra effort and considerable planning. The immediate results may be minimal.

Here is a completely non-exhaustive list of additional benefits to children serving:

- **Kids who serve** learn that a life of following Christ prioritizes others.
- **Kids who serve** learn that God has gifted them to do good works.
- **Kids who serve** learn to experience church rather than consume as spectators only.

An ultimate example would be for kids to serve alongside their parents. If your church allows, ask if you can bring your older child or teen to assist you in a preschool class. Or bring your child to help prepare for VBS. The more active parents are in the church, the more opportunities will naturally occur for kids to serve.

The greatest benefit of course won't be realized until those kids become young adults living lives of faith. Like regular Bible reading, consistency over time counts. Puberty doesn't happen overnight. Maturation isn't an isolated event. Adding serving within the church to the spiritual growth tool kit you employ in your home and program within your church is both a noticeable and effective way to make a difference in the people our sons and daughters become. The example they set for us in serving might just hold us accountable and inspire even greater service in us along the way.

33%
of kids regularly served at church.
(Nothing Less Study)

+ POSITIVE INFLUENCER

A child who listened primarily to Christian music while growing up has 7.5% stronger spiritual health as a young adult.

– NEGATIVE INFLUENCER

A child who regularly listened to secular/popular music while growing up has 2.5% lower spiritual health as a young adult.[23]

MUSIC

Another influencer with moderate impact is primarily listening to Christian music while growing up is as influential as spending time in prayer or serving in the church. This moderate impact indicator offers 7.5 percent stronger spiritual health as a young adult.

Moving into influencers with smaller impact, we have an opposite but not quite equal indicator; a child who regularly listens to only secular or popular music while growing up has 2.5 percent lower spiritual health. It would seem, simply looking at numbers, that the positive effects of Christian music are more powerful than even the negative effects of contrasting tunes.

In some ways, is comparing Christian and secular music like comparing carrots and cookies? As parents, do we simply want to ensure that our kids get more veggies than they do sugary carbs? Or is it more than that? Are we really winning as parents if we simply provide more Christian music than we allow secular? At some point, our kids have to learn the why behind what we do.

More research would be necessary to clarify why the presence of Christian music has such a strong positive effect. Is it the way that music emotes? Is it the lyrical reminder of God's good news? Is it the way that the listener can participate? Is it the fact that it's accessibility helps us remain connected to our faith throughout the week? Plus, note that what one person defines as Christian music may differ substantially from another. Christian music may be defined as hymns to one person, while it may be contemporary Christian radio to another.

Ultimately, even without added research, we know an important why. It's found in a line from a timeless Christian classic, "The Bible tells me so." Yes, that lyric from "Jesus Loves Me" references how we can know with certainty that Jesus does indeed love us, but it also reminds us that all Scripture is true, including this verse:

"Finally brothers and sisters, whatever is true, whatever is honorable, whatever is just, whatever is pure, whatever is lovely, whatever is commendable—if there is any moral excellence and if there is anything praiseworthy—dwell on these things" (Philippians 4:8).

Christian lyrics yield a positive spiritual health outcome while secular lyrics do not because what goes in will indeed come out. While not part of this particular research, parents will undoubtedly ask if this axiom includes other forms of media. The concept certainly seems true, but what is the actual value of Christian music in particular?

First, theology. Lyrics from biblical texts can teach and reinforce the truths of our faith. Song lyrics can help us remember Bible verses, making Psalm 119:11 come to life: *"I have treasured your word in my heart so that I may not sin against you."* Whether Christian or secular, conversations sparked by popular media can be an important way for parents and church leaders to continually convey doctrine and theology.

Second, devotion. Music can offer us chances to pray, praise, contemplate, hear, and even speak to God. Lyrics don't just educate. They give children a chance to imitate the heartbeat of a Christ-following God worshiper. Music can tell us who God is and give us a platform to recognize and thank Him for it.

So how do parents grapple with secular music and other forms of popular media being so pervasive in our culture? Do we only allow them to hear songs about Jesus? Perhaps we can give them Christian music and other forms of Christian media in larger doses, while also equipping them with tools to evaluate the secular ones.

Demonstrating to kids how faith can be applicable in everyday life includes conversations about the inherently Christ-honoring forms of media we choose. It also involves the inherently not Christ-honoring forms that we sometimes enjoy and are often exposed to. Both can present incredible fodder for theological conversations and preparing your child for the day he prepares his own playlist.[24]

22% of kids listened to primarliy Christian music. (Nothing Less Study)

58% of kids listened primarily to secular or popular music. (Nothing Less Study)

5

A child who participated in mission trips while growing up has 6.25% stronger spiritual health as a young adult.[25]

MISSIONS

Here's where the findings become shocking. This next item from the influencers with moderate impact is not a surprise in and of itself, but when compared to our earlier list of presuppositions (i.e. family dinners, one-on-one outings, emphasizing grace and forgiveness, and the like), we realize items that most of us were certain would top the charts for lifelong spiritual influence showed no impact overall. This next finding is one that we may not naturally guess but presents an incredible opportunity.

A child who participated in missions trips or projects while growing up has 6.25 percent stronger spiritual health as a young adult.

Missions education may be common in your children's ministry programming and even your discussions at home. Missions trips may be common, but most likely for adults and students already advancing through middle and high school. Because young adults who remain connected to the church, thriving in their commitment to Christ, share a background in actual missions trips, parents and church leaders can step in to make this endeavor possible for kids in your church.

What if, instead of waiting to introduce actual missions trip experiences to kids when they are older, we planned mission trip experiences in their lives like DNA from the beginning? There are benefits, even beyond the long lasting effects on their individual lives as they grow up.

THE "WHY" BEHIND MISSIONS FOR KIDS:

A child's worldview is almost fully formed by age 12.[26] That means that before a child even enters adolescence, her understanding of the world and how it functions is nearly complete. Missions for kids gives them a chance to decentralize and realize that there are others in the world who live with significant needs. Missions offers kids a chance to be part of a team, show compassion to others, obey the commands of God, and experience the body of Christ in a hands-on way. It allows them to see and experience the gifts that God gives believers in action. It's a tactile learning environment where kids grow by doing.

Before a child ever goes on a mission trip, parents and ministry leaders can begin fostering a love for the unreached and under-served. Learning about the community and world around them is a huge step in the right direction. Kids of all ages can pray for others to know Jesus. They can learn how to share their faith as they grow older. Ultimately, we want them to have a heart for the nations and be the future goers and senders. It begins now.

THE "HOW" BEHIND MISSIONS FOR KIDS:

Logistics tend to be where we logically get off the train concerning kids serving. There are leadership, safety, and organizational components at play that simply don't require as much attention when involving adults. Children serving on mission will require much more work, which could indicate just how much greater the reward will be.

Begin knowing that a missions trip involving children really is a family missions trip. Missional experiences with young children should always involve their primary caregivers. Traveling with children has limitations. Consider keeping any driving distances and flying distances to within three to six hours. That automatically limits locations. Once you land on a place, consider the importance of pace. While adults or teens may be accustomed to spending eigh-teen hour days serving, kids will need regular opportunities to rest, regroup, and digest what they are doing and learning. Taking along ministry veterans who work well with children will create built-in

27%
of kids participated in church mission trips or projects.
(Nothing Less Study)

thresholds of patience and provide the necessary kid communication skills you will likely need to direct kids and their parents. In some cases, know that the child's first missions trip experience may be the parents' first missions trip experience too.

The list of necessary details goes on and on, and in some ways is very specific to the location you serve and the type of ministry you intend to perform. Keep in mind this final axiom. Just as important, if not slightly more so, than the work you do with kids is the work God does in them. While you can indeed accomplish much for the kingdom of God by His power, even with young kids, your goal as a parent or church ministry leader is to foster a love for missions, for others, and for God in the hearts of the kids themselves.

Think back to a missional experience that shaped and changed you. Imagine if it had come during your early, formative years. That's what missions does in kids. According to our Nothing Less study, the impact of those missions trip experiences is far-reaching and effective for raising Christ-centered adults.

LIFE CHANGING:
85% YOUTH REPORTED
FEELING MORE LOVED BY GOD
AFTER GOING ON A SHORT-TERM MISSION TRIP. THE MAJORITY SAID **IT CHANGED THEIR LIFE** IN SOME WAY, INCLUDING LEARNING MORE ABOUT POVERTY, JUSTICE, OR THE WORLD, INCREASING COMPASSION, DEEPENING OR ENRICHING **THEIR FAITH.**

6

INTEREST LEVEL IN CHURCH

Are you seeing the future of your investment? Marveling at how quickly your 5 year old learned to read her Bible and how quickly she devoured the Minor Prophets? Creating online scrapbooks from 12 years of consecutive missions trips to various countries in Central and South America? Starting your savings account to pay for seminary for your future young adult children who will obviously want to go?

There is some saying about counting chickens before they hatch. It's necessary now for us to note that not all of the top ten predictors of spiritual health yield a positive impact. We touched on this in our section on Christian music, noting that listening to primarily popular or secular music negatively affected overall spiritual condition in young adults. Now, we must examine factors weighing in even more negatively on overall results.

What if it isn't as easy as praying and reading the Bible regularly and programming all our radio station playlists to Christian tunes? What if it isn't as simple as providing opportunities for mission trips to be part of your child's Christian development? Let's revisit one of our earlier biblical principles. While it remains our job to plant and water, only God gives growth. According to Paul, our role matters only a little in terms of growth.

"So then neither the one who plants nor the one who waters is anything, but only God who gives the growth" (1 Corinthians 3:7).

What if you incorporate all of those things that trend toward positive results, but your child simply doesn't want to participate? What if you son resents participation in church programming and even balks at basic attendance? What if your daughter cringes at daily spiritual disciplines and rebels against activities of faith in the home?

⊖ NEGATIVE INFLUENCER

A teen who did not want to go to church has 5% lower spiritual health as a young adult.

⊖ NEGATIVE INFLUENCER

A child who was rebellious while growing up has 3.75% lower spiritual health as a young adult.[27]

According to our Nothing Less research, a child who was rebellious while growing up has 3.75 percent lower spiritual health as a young adult. A teen who did not want to go to church has 5% lower spiritual health.

Before we dive into ideas for parents and leaders to address this pressing challenge present in so many families, we need to pause for a disclaimer. For this statistic regarding interest level in church to have registered among our top tiers of spiritual condition predictors, it must be widespread. Take at least some form of comfort in that if you are a mom or dad battling your own rebellious child who doesn't want to be part of church, you are not alone. Not only does God promise to be with you, there are other parents going through similar struggles. The enemy would like for you to wear the shame of failure and live under the threat of isolation. He would have you believe lies like, "This is all your fault," and "No other well-meaning Christian parent is dealing with this." This statistic bubbled to the surface of common factors because it is just that—common.

WHAT CAN PARENTS DO TO HELP?

Parents should first feel complete freedom to know and parent their own kids without fear of judgment from other Christians.

Next, parents should feel permission to know their own kids and manage their own families. In some seasons, parents might need to press in and set boundaries and expectations for children. In other seasons, parents might need to demonstrate grace and exercise sensitivity to their children's busyness, fears, and motivations.

Finally, parents should seek and trust in the wisdom of the Holy Spirit to direct their parenting plan in these tough moments.

"EVEN THE VERY BEST PARENT IN THE UNIVERSE — GOD HIMSELF — HAS REBELLIOUS CHILDREN (ISAIAH 1:2–3). SO DON'T LET SATAN LOAD YOU DOWN WITH FAITH-DESTROYING GUILT GREATER THAN YOU CAN BEAR OR SHOULD BEAR." –JOHN PIPER

"It is not
our work
to make men
believe:
that is the work of the
Holy Spirit."

–D.L. MOODY

WHAT CAN CHURCH LEADERS DO?

First, church leaders should create grace-filled environments where parents can be open about the challenges they face without threat of judgment or fear of labels. Open lines of communication between ministry leaders and parents are a must.

Next, church leaders should work to ensure that all of the volunteers leading out in ministry are called to serve and excited to be there themselves. In some cases, the perception from children might be that the volunteers don't enjoy leading and investing, so why should kids enjoy being present and participating?

Church leaders can also fine-tune and evaluate programming to make sure it really is effectively reaching and teaching children. Leaders should ask themselves, "Does our programming involve multiple types of learning, work to foster relationships among partic-ipants in peer groups, and involve adults truly valuing and investing in kids and students?" This idea of relational connections will surface again as we examine yet another spiritual condition predictor.

Both parents and ministry leaders should investigate the "why" behind a rebellious child's actions and the "why" behind a child or student's resistance. While there may be common excuses, each individual heart can be nurtured in unique ways. The important thing to remember is to never give up. It's never too late for a prodigal to come home. Trust in God's timing.

22%
of kids did not want to go to church as a teen.
(Nothing Less Study)

16%
of kids were rebellious growing up.
(Nothing Less Study)

INFLUENCE BY OTHERS

"The one who walks with the wise will become wise, but a companion of fools will suffer harm" (Proverbs 13:20).

In a manner of speaking, this spiritual condition predictor is one that we trend toward observing the negative rather than the positive outcomes. The writer of Proverbs 13:20 presents both sides of the coin, but the latter trumps the former more often than not in our attention spans. For our purposes now, we are channeling our inner optimists and observing the truly positive possibilities.

Both of the following smaller impact predictors of positive spiritual outcomes in young adults play well together.

A child whose best friend was an influence to follow Christ while growing up has a 5% higher spiritual health as a young adult.

A child who connected with several adults at church who intentionally invested in her spiritually and personally while growing up has 3.75 percent higher spiritual health as a young adult.

Why do we hear the word influence regarding our kids and automatically insert the word *bad* in front of it? As parents and ministry leaders, we are keenly aware of the many layers of negative influences that war for our children's attention. Take a deep breath and spend the next few moments fully realizing the alternative power of positive influences in your kids' lives.

We all know that relationships in the context of church have the potential to create a gravitational pull toward many good things. Friendships offer accountability and support. Mentoring provides discipleship and training. Children develop relationships through familiarity over time, play, and shared stories. Those friendships can offer a positive influence as children hear and respond to Christ.

➕ POSITIVE INFLUENCER

A child whose best friend was an influence to follow Christ while growing up has 5% stronger spiritual health as a young adult.

➕ POSITIVE INFLUENCER

A child who connected with several adults at church who intentionally invested in them spiritually and personally while growing up has 3.75% stronger spiritual health as a young adult.[28]

On the other hand, blindly walking a child through the process of trusting Jesus as Savior and being baptized simply because his friend made a similar decision is careless. Allowing the spiritual growth of others to inspire and prompt your child is another story. Leveraging those moments to deepen spiritual conversations with your children is akin to seizing another great opportunity to share the gospel.

When research about young adults asserts that a having a close friend at church strengthens spiritual connections, it's a good idea for parents and church leaders to create environments where such friendships can flourish.

If we know that friendships are going to be influential, parents can and should do whatever it takes to help their children find friendships that will have a positive impact. As if there aren't enough reasons for adults to fully engage in the life of the church, here we have another: the more active Mom and Dad are, the more close relationships they can form. The more relationships Mom and Dad have, the more parents know of potential friends and playmates for their own children. Then families can engage in actually doing life together and provide more opportunities for shared experiences, play, learning, and increased familiarity. It's a cycle that continues to give. Involvement on parents' part is also the best way to be forewarned of any friendships that would benefit from increased boundaries rather than increased access.

Beyond peer influences, young adults surveyed indicate the power of other adults in their lives who made an intentional investment. Parents are certainly the primary disciple-makers of their kids, but they are not the only disciple-makers of their kids. Here's another moment where parental involvement in the life of the church comes to the rescue. The more involved parents are, the more likely they are to have enhanced relationships with other adults who could serve as mentors and investors in the lives of their own kids. In this

12%
of kids had a best friend who influenced them to follow Christ.
(Nothing Less Study)

41%
of kids connected with several adults at church who intentionally invested in them spiritually and personally while growing up.
(Nothing Less Study)

THE MORE
INVOLVED
PARENTS ARE,
THE MORE LIKELY
THEY ARE TO
HAVE ENHANCED
RELATIONSHIPS
WITH OTHER
ADULTS WHO
COULD SERVE AS
MENTORS AND
INVESTORS IN THE
LIVES OF THEIR
OWN KIDS.

manner, parents are given the opportunity to handpick men and women to pour into their kids and speak into the family's life.

As moms and dads, it's not enough to know our kids. We need to know the people who have the power to positively influence them. Among all of the spiritual condition predictors, the idea of influence was woven into several. In this case, both peers and other adults matter. As parents and ministry leaders, we want to do all we can to ensure our kids have positive Christ-centered friendships as well as godly men and women to serve as their mentors.

Nothing less for me.

8

INFLUENCE BY PARENTS

This significant predictor is the one we long for most: confirmation that we as parents do indeed make a lasting difference in the lives of our kids. According to our Nothing Less research, this particular line item is not as noteworthy as Bible reading, prayer, or even peer friendships, but two specific actions parents can take register as equal smaller impact predictors.

Children whose parents typically asked their forgiveness when they messed up has 2.5 percent higher spiritual health as a young adult.

A child whose parents typically pointed out biblical principles in everyday life has 2.5 percent higher spiritual health as a young adult.

Wait? We already let the proverbial cat out of the imaginary bag on both of these predictors in an earlier section, right? Yes. Both were exposed as actionable items for parents in the section marked, "What can the family do?"

But why these two specific actions? Ultimately, we know that the role of parents has tentacles into each of the top 10 predictors. After all, parents play a role in regular Bible reading, prayer, friendship fostering, music, serving, and missions. Why did these two parental involvement pieces rise to the top of the list, beating out other items that we more naturally would have assumed (enter family dinner again)?

Here's at least one suggestion as to why these traits both matter: They serve as symbols for two of the most important components of faith. So naturally, when being surveyed regarding their own commitment to Christ, specific actions performed by parents that serve as visual representations of core theological truths surfaced with clarity.

Asking forgiveness:

"According to the law almost everything is purified with blood, and without the shedding of blood there is no forgiveness" (Hebrews 9:22).

We love to talk about how good things from God like grace and salvation are free. To us, that's true. To Him, not so much. Grace was costly. Jesus spent His life to afford it for us. Grace and forgiveness are available at no charge to us, certainly, but Jesus paid the ultimate price.

When parents are willing to ask forgiveness, they highlight again and again our most essential necessity. We're all sinners in desperate need of God's gracious forgiveness. Parents assuming a posture of humility by admitting their own faults send a powerful message to their children. Forgiveness is the current by which salvation flows. What could offer more lifelong spiritual impact in the development of a child than a parent who acknowledged regularly the need for it?

Pointing out truth:

"For this reason also, since the day we heard this, we haven't stopped praying for you. We are asking that you may be filled with the knowledge of his will in all wisdom and spiritual understanding, so that you may walk worthy of the Lord, fully pleasing to him: bearing fruit in every good work and growing in the knowledge of God" (Colossians 1:9-10).

Paul's prayer request on behalf of Colossian believers is a good one to pray for each other and a great one to pray for our children. As parents and church ministry leaders, we should be diligently asking the God of this great universe to fill our kids up with the knowledge of His will. We should beg of God to give them wisdom and spiritual understanding so that they can walk worthy of their calling and bear fruit in daily discipleship.

57%
of parents pointed out biblical principles in everyday life.
(Nothing Less Study)

54%
of parents asked forgiveness when they messed up.
(Nothing Less Study)

Take a moment to emphasize the idea of spiritual understanding. That's seeing the world with a biblical lens. It's understanding worldwide news, and even your own tough circumstance, through the bigger picture of the gospel. It's seeing and seizing every opportunity around you to know God better. As parents and church leaders, our goal is to pray that and be that for our kids. Pointing out biblical truths in everyday life is a tutorial for spiritual understanding. It's doing our part to raise kids with a biblical worldview keen on knowing God better and better each day.

Yes, parents have unlimited influence. We are the trump card of influence in our kids' lives with a role to play in each and every one of the top predictors. In some ways that's a great deal of pressure. By God's grace, it's an even greater deal of opportunity. By asking forgiveness when needed and pointing out biblical principles whenever and wherever we can, we're equipping them with two tools they'll need to function as Christ-followers.

The first tool is humility. We need God but don't deserve Him. Forgiveness is required. The second tool is eyesight. We need spiritual eyesight in order to truly follow Him. May we all pass along both of these great legacy tools to our kids!

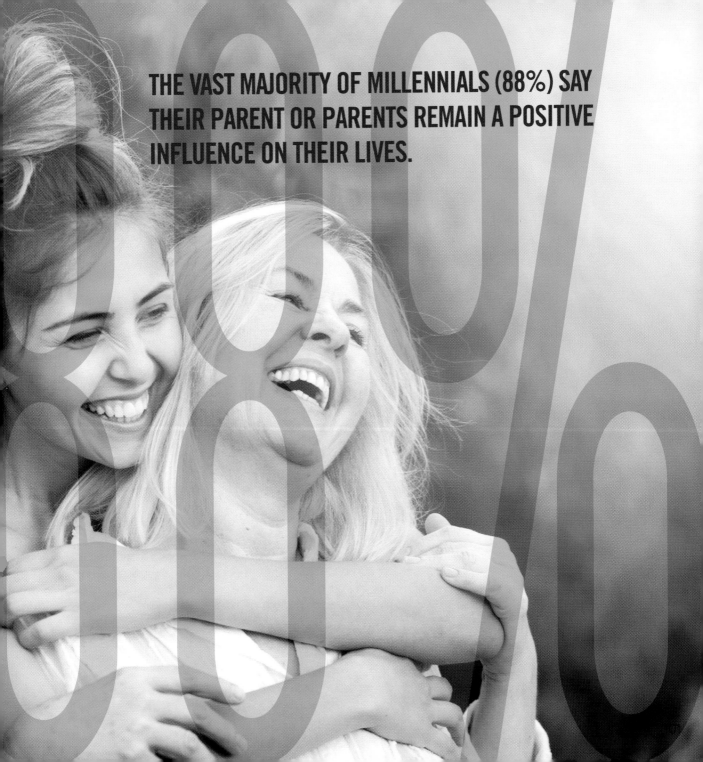

THE VAST MAJORITY OF MILLENNIALS (88%) SAY THEIR PARENT OR PARENTS REMAIN A POSITIVE INFLUENCE ON THEIR LIVES.

9

➕ POSITIVE INFLUENCER

Girls have a 3.75% stronger spiritual health as a young adult.

➕ POSITIVE INFLUENCER

For each sibling a child has, he or she has a 1.25% stronger spiritual level as a young adult.[30]

GENDER AND SIBLINGS

Couldn't we have guessed it? There had to be at least one, maybe two, items in the list of top ten influencers completely outside the realm of human control, and that is a good thing. Rounding out the list of smaller impact significant predictors of positive spiritual outcomes in young adults are two such items.

Girls have 3.75 percent higher spiritual health as young adults.

So, simply being female is linked to positive results when it comes to living a faith-filled life as a young adult. The results of being a female don't have nearly the overall impact as regularly reading the Bible or praying, but it did make the list. Of course, while being female offers an enhanced chance at spiritual health into adulthood, the opposite side of the statistic must come under investigation.

The study did *not* say that being male has a negative effect. In fact, it could be very benign, neutral, or of no effect at all. We can't jump to any additional conclusion other than to report that girls have a statistically higher chance of spiritual health in young adulthood simply by nature of growing up female.

Churches should then only minister to young girls, thereby enhancing their overall level of successful kingdom impact, right? Of course not! Parents of girls should continue to lean into the same spiritual health predictors throughout the childhood of their young girls. Get young girls reading their Bibles. Help them develop healthy habits of regular prayer. Provide mentors and opportunities for healthy friendships. Give them chances to discover their gifts, serve the body, and be on mission. Do the same for boys, but with an extra dose of prayer for the young men in your ministry to beat any uncomfortable odds.

In addition to gender, the size of a person's family also landed squarely in tier three as a significant indicator of spiritual health.

For each sibling a child has, he has 1.25 percent higher spiritual health as a young adult. So, in order to achieve the same level of enhancement as regularly studying the Word, a person needs a minimum of 9 siblings. Of course, it would be less expensive and less taxing to focus on regular Bible reading.

Why is it that additional siblings can be linked to higher spiritual condition? Just a few unsubstantiated guesses might come into play:

1 **Perhaps children with more siblings** learn the value of community in a more concentrated setting.

2 **Perhaps children with more siblings** learn the value of service and sharing as part of their family DNA.

3 **Perhaps children with more siblings** trend toward other healthy behaviors such as regular church attendance and even others that don't make the list of significant predictors but lend support to the items that did. For example, family dinner time is not a top predictor; however, that quality time around the table could provide the perfect setting for moms and dads to point out biblical principles and pray together as a family.

Ultimately, these two predictors being so concretely out of our hands does us an incredible favor. They remind us as parents and ministry leaders, once again, that all of this really is in God's hands. When we have increased dependence on Him, we'll do a far better job leading out in any of the capacities He's calling us to lead. For instance, we as parents will approach our prayer life, Bible emphasis, and overall influence from an open-handed position of humility. If gender and even number of kids—being outside of our control—fosters humility and greater dependence on God among us, that is an overall positive effect worth noting and leveraging.

10

For each drop in frequency of family church service attendance while growing up, a young adult has a corresponding 1.25% drop in spiritual health.[31]

CHURCH ATTENDANCE

"When I was young, my parents took me to church every time the doors were open."

No one is going to suggest or suppose that perfect church attendance in childhood is a direct link to spiritual health in young adults. If so, we would have spent far less time exposing the value of God's Word and devotional family time and gone straight to star charts and incentives to get kids in our church doors.

What is the link and what can we do about it?

According to Pew Research, only 35% of American Christians find "attending religious services" to be an essential part of what it means to be a Christian. That's an important distinction that may have little or no bearing on a person's spiritual health. Note the word *may*. More likely, a person's commitment to attending services probably has a significant effect on how he connects with and follows Christ. However, it's just not the purpose of this data. What is part of the data is the effect of regular family participation for kids over the long haul of their journey into young adulthood. Those effects can be noted.

For each drop in frequency of family church service attendance while growing up, a young adult has a corresponding 1.25 percent drop on spiritual health.

That means every time a family dropped in frequency, the benefit of one more sibling was canceled out. Imagine trying to have another kid every time you determined to attend church less often in order to keep up. That is almost as ludicrous as trying to be present in church every single time doors are unlocked. The purpose of focusing on attendance isn't to foster legalism or create pharisaical-style rules too burdensome for us to handle.

Ultimately, the purpose here is to note that a widespread American trend is having an effect, and our children are paying the price. It makes sense when you think about it. Families who attend less often are probably less likely to serve regularly or connect with missions teams serving abroad. However, they may still be hitting grand slam home runs in Bible reading and prayer but missing the other spiritual condition influencers along the way.

While the number of evangelical churchgoers itself is stable, the definition of regular church attendance has changed. Remember, there is no plumb line for church attendance patterns that do or do not experience a drop in spiritual condition. The 1.25 percent drop occurs with each drop in frequency. Cumulatively, that number could be much higher. A high school graduate who experienced four or five drops in the frequency of church attendance throughout his school years has a 5 to 6.25 percent lower rate of spiritual health return in young adulthood.

For parents, we must begin by asking ourselves if those odds are worth the risk when it comes to the future of our children and potential grandchildren. For church leaders, we must begin by asking ourselves if we are doing everything within our ministry parameters to educate parents and partner together for the good of the next generation.

We should all be seated for the next two Bible verses. Warning: these two verses from Judges might be the scariest verses in all the Bible.

> "That whole generation was also gathered to their ancestors. After them another generation rose up who did not know the LORD or the works he had done for Israel" (Judges 2:10).

> "In those days there was no king in Israel; everyone did whatever seemed right to him" (Judges 21:25).

71%
of parents said their families attended church at least once a week as their children were growing up. (Nothing Less Study)

Collectively, we have to shout together, "Not on our watch!" We refuse to be the generation of parents and ministry leaders who allowed an entire generation of kids to come up behind our ranks without faith in God granted to us through the gospel truth of His Son, Jesus. We refuse to be the generation who steps aside in fear while a new generation operates according to their own evil desires, failing to recognize that we have a King and His name is Jesus. We know too well that a life lived doing whatever we want is the fastest way to ruin. Abundance, to the world's chagrin, is only found in Jesus. We as parents and ministry leaders have the awesome task and incredible privilege of raising kids to know Jesus and know Him well. If the significant predictors and spiritual condition data found in these studies can help, then bring it on.

Nothing less
will light up
my whole
entire heart.

WHAT CAN PARENTS DO?

THE PARENT INFLUENCERS

"At the end of the day, our children alone must choose whether they will follow Christ. But as parents, we long to do everything we can to encourage them to follow Him. So we looked at which parenting practices best predict this choice."
—Scott McConnell, Executive Director of LifeWay Research

When God called His people out of slavery in Egypt, they had no idea the journey He would be taking them on. Imagine the incredible spiritual high everyone must have felt just three miles past the parting of the Red Sea. They even sang about it. It's a whole chapter—Exodus 14 to be exact. Now fast-forward three days. There was no water. Complaining, grumbling, and confusion had set in.

This situation is not unlike the journey of parenthood. There are those moments when everything just feels so miraculous that you want to break into song. They are typically, and sometimes immediately, followed up by moments with no win in sight. Equally, understanding that so much of the research reveals things that are within our influence but outside of our control is a hard line to walk.

DISCOVERING THE PARENT INFLUENCERS

Moses had incredible influence but could in no way control the whining or the idolatry people were so prone to seek. So goes much of the research we have examined so far. Many of the options young adults could have indicated as primary childhood predictors of spiritual health were based on *childhood behavior*. We went back through the research again and ran the numbers *removing all indicators of spiritual health based on childhood behaviors.* Removing those, the impact of parental involvement becomes more clear.

Why do so? Because many of the characteristics most predictive of spiritual condition relate to *child habits*, the influence of parental practices are obscured. Omitting child-controlled items allows for a greater understanding of parenting practices.

Consider the 9 positive influencers of parents in the graphic on page 111.

NINE THINGS PARENTS CAN DO TO INFLUENCE THE LONG-TERM SPIRITUAL CONDITION OF THEIR KIDS

When child-controlled behaviors were removed, leaving only parent behaviors, these nine emerged as statistically significant.

1. Parents participated in missions trips as a family as their kids were growing up.

2. Parents participated in ministry or service projects with their kids as they were growing up.

3. Parents frequently shared Christ with unbelievers as their kids were growing up.

4. Parents personally read the Bible several times a week or more as their kids were growing up.

5. Parents encouraged teen children to serve in the church.

6. Parents typically asked forgiveness when they messed up as their children were growing up.

7. Parents encouraged their children's own unique talents and interests as they grew up.

8. Parents attended churches that emphasized what the Bible says as their kids were growing up.

9. Parents taught their children to tithe as their kids were growing up.

Did you catch all of these great confirmations and correlations? We've already promoted and evaluated several of these key, positive, statistically significant predictors when our options included childhood habits. However, notice how many of these parent practices involve hands-on parental involvement? All of them! As you consider possible changes to your parenting in light of this research, think back to our discussion about how Christians in our society today tend to outsource more of their children's spiritual development than they realize. This list reveals that your impact is multiplied when you are right beside your kids growing in faith and serving together. Let's zero in more closely on a few of these parent practices.

First, raising the bar of **sharing one's faith with others** is a way to demonstrate personal evangelism in the family. Apparently, young adults with higher Spiritual Condition Scores noted that their parents actively shared Christ with others. It stands to reason that if parents were consistent in the biblical command to share the gospel outside of the home, they would also regularly seize opportunities within the home. Perhaps that forms a loose connection to the smaller impact predictor of parents who pointed out biblical truths in everyday life. Either way, we know as committed Christ-followers that sharing Jesus with others matters for the kingdom's sake. Now we also know it matters in the long-term desire of the children we raise to be Christ followers into adulthood. Demonstrating personal evangelism has a far reaching impact, almost as high as that of parents taking missions trips and equal to participating in service opportunities with their kids.

Next, **encouraging children's unique talents** made the cut. Understanding what we saw from the data regarding the effects of children being engaged in serving opportunities within the church, we shouldn't be surprised that the identification of talent, and perhaps even spiritual gifts, helps our children to grow. Specifically for parents, serving with our kids and encouraging teens to serve also rose above other less significant predictors.

"THE SINGLE GREATEST REASON WHY WE ARE LOSING A GENERATION IS BECAUSE THE HOME IS NO LONGER THE PLACE OF THE TRANSFERENCE OF THE FAITH. WE LIVE IN A DAY OF 'OUTSOURCING'... TODAY, WE HAVE A GENERATION OF PEOPLE THAT OUTSOURCE THEIR KIDS."
—TONY EVANS

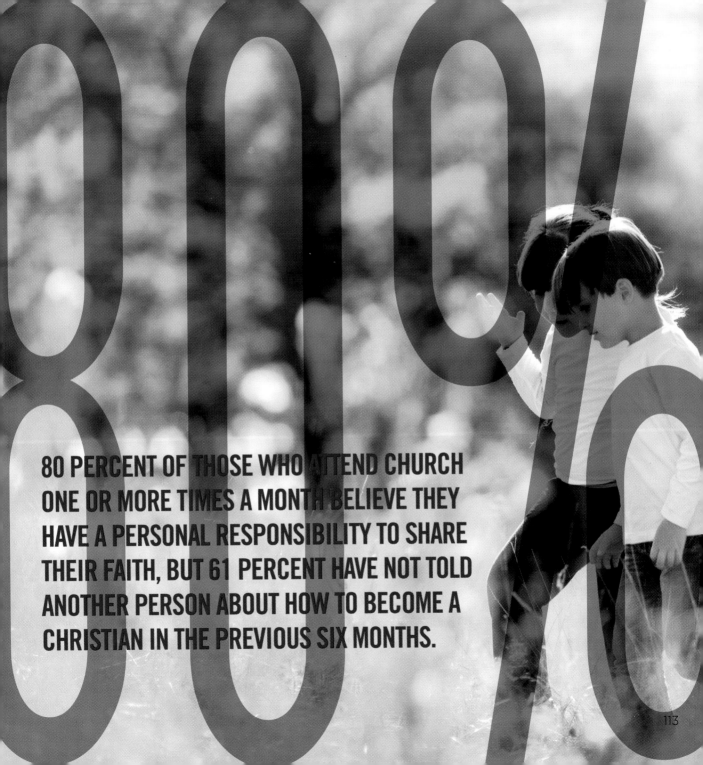

80 PERCENT OF THOSE WHO ATTEND CHURCH ONE OR MORE TIMES A MONTH BELIEVE THEY HAVE A PERSONAL RESPONSIBILITY TO SHARE THEIR FAITH, BUT 61 PERCENT HAVE NOT TOLD ANOTHER PERSON ABOUT HOW TO BECOME A CHRISTIAN IN THE PREVIOUS SIX MONTHS.

ONLY 9% OF CHURCHGOERS STRONGLY AGREE WITH THE STATEMENT "I INTENTIONALLY GIVE UP CERTAIN PURCHASES SO I CAN USE THAT MONEY FOR OTHERS."

Fostering the Christian identity of children as created uniquely by a wonderful God, in His own image, should be a bold parenting priority. Consider briefly the role of parents as encouragers of their children—athletically, academically, and artistically. What if identifying special gifts and abilities also included finding ways that our kids' talents, interests, and gifting could be used in ministry? It's easy to see why having parents who identified and encouraged talents and illustrated how they might be used in ministry would have a spiritually significant impact on young adults.

Finally, **teaching your children to tithe**, to give God back a tenth of all earnings, stands out as a significant practice for parents that was not found in the previous child behavior-related data.

Jesus' words in Matthew 6:21, *"For where your treasure is, there your heart will be also,"* aren't specifically in reference to presenting a tithe, but they speak directly to our material wealth and possessions. A good goal for any parents, particularly God-honoring ones, is raising kids who are free from the trappings of materialism. That's a tall task in this world. Tithing can help. When we teach our kids the biblical practice of tithing, and even the importance of going beyond a tenth, we offer our kids the following benefits:

First, we give them a regular, repetitive chance to submit to the leadership of Christ in a concrete way. Paychecks come once a week, once every two weeks, or once a month. Tithing off the top then gives you multiple opportunities each month to physically say to God, "I trust you. What I have is yours. I submit to your will and way in my life. This portion is an act of gratitude today."

Second, when we teach tithing, we set an automatic cap on spending. If our kids grow up with a mindset of only living on 80% of their resources because they give and save equal measures of the other 20%, we've already helped them avoid the trap of materialism and debt-fueled living that plagues so many others.

Finally, teaching our kids tithing helps them develop a habit at a young age that could be far more difficult to develop as adults. It's far easier for kids to learn a new language than adults. The habits we form early are often the ones that stick. Teaching our kids to tithe forms a healthy habit early on that could indeed follow them into adulthood and yield spiritual results throughout their lives.

There are likely even more practical and spiritual benefits to tithing not addressed here. Suffice it to say that tithing emphasized in the home during childhood has an impact on the spiritual health of young adults, and that's reason enough to employ the practice as a parent.[32]

NOTING THE NEGATIVE PARENT INFLUENCERS

Sadly, we must also consider the negative influences of parenting practices on overall spiritual condition scores in young adults. The following triad of connected behaviors offered a negative impact:

1. Parents allowed **teens to choose if they wanted to attend church**.

2. Each **drop in frequency of family church attendance** as kids were growing up.

3. Each **drop in frequency of family devotionals** as kids were growing up.

To some degree, each of these negative influences is part of a larger ripple effect. According to additional research, most Americans (including Christians) believe that the purpose of life is to find fulfillment by discovering yourself and pursuing whatever makes you happy. If that ideal manifests itself in families and parenting, which we know it does, teens are free to explore fulfillment options elsewhere. The world is happy to step in and provide alternatives.

As perception of our purpose in life continues to drift away from Christian values and purpose oriented under divine order and into the realm of self-interest, it's no wonder that family participation in devotional activities and church attendance wanes.

People do what they value. People engage what they perceive will achieve their highest goal. Because we can easily note how each drop in frequency of church attendance and family devotion manifests itself negatively in the spiritual health of young adults, it's not a hard leap to admit that those battles originally began in childhood and in the teenage years. If culture holds the pursuit of personal desires as the highest esteem, it's no wonder that parents might allow teens to neglect the church in favor of fulfillment elsewhere.

FINDING PERSPECTIVE

Ultimately, it's always important to remember that oven temperatures may vary. Every pre-made brownie mix you've ever purchased reminds you that your oven may indeed be different from every other test kitchen oven used in the development of that recipe. As parents, we can create the best possible environments for our children to engage positive spiritual disciplines, but at the end of the day, we can't ensure or enforce salvation and sanctification. As parents, we can follow the best laid plans and exhibit all the right behaviors regarding these additional 12 conditional influencers (9 positive and 3 negative) and still come up with results far more influenced by other outside factors. To put it plainly, we can read all the books we want on parenting, but guess who hasn't read any of them? Our children! That's why parenting is an exercise in faith and reliance.

We are on a journey. It can be a wilderness. What God will provide is leadership and lordship for every single step. He'll give wisdom when we seek it and restoration when we undoubtedly mess up and need it. That's where section 5 of this resource will take us. Journey on.

AS PARENTS, WE CAN CREATE THE BEST POSSIBLE ENVIRONMENTS FOR OUR CHILDREN TO ENGAGE POSITIVE SPIRITUAL DISCIPLINES, BUT AT THE END OF THE DAY, WE CAN'T ENSURE OR ENFORCE SALVATION AND SANCTIFICATION.

5

YOU CAN DO THIS!

LISTEN

In the Old Testament, for the newly rescued Israelite, the most important Hebrew word was *shema*. We tend to translate it as the command "hear" or "listen" in English when, in fact, it carries multiple definitions. *Shema* also means "obey." For the Israelite, hearing from God and obeying God was one and the same. In fact, you did not hear God unless you obeyed Him.

> *"Listen, Israel: The LORD our God, the LORD is one. Love the LORD your God with all your heart, with all your soul, and with all your strength. These words that I am giving you today are to be in your heart. Repeat them to your children. Talk about them when you sit in your house and when you walk along the road, when you lie down and when you get up. Bind them as a sign on your hand and let them be a symbol on your forehead. Write them on the doorposts of your house and on your city gates" (Deuteronomy 6:4-9).*

We often refer to Jesus' words in Matthew 22:37-38 as the Great Commandments. Christ wasn't offering new truth unfamiliar to the Jewish listener. He was quoting the words of Moses in Deuteronomy 6:5. What exactly was Israel to hear and do? Love God with absolutely everything. In today's terms, we would understand the head or the mind to be the source of governance and decision-making in a person's life. For the ancient Hebrew learner, that source of leadership in life was the heart. Loving God with everything that you are and basing all of your decisions on His guidance is the primary command and foremost expression of faith. That's why it mattered that the words of God transmitted through Moses made their home in the hearts of the Israelites.

What was next? Passing that faith on to the next generation. Notice how Moses didn't pause and move from the entire community of faith ("Listen, Israel") to narrow his address to only parents. The entire extended community of God's people remained Moses' audience. That means that it wasn't just the role of biological mom

Nothing less for me.
Or Nana either.

and dad to raise children who knew, trusted, and followed God. It was the burden of the entire community of rescued slaves to ensure that new generations grew up fully immersed in the story of God.

Breathe a sigh of relief, Mom. Slow your heartbeat, Dad. While you are called and equipped by God Almighty to pour Christ into your children, you are not alone. God has purposed a community of faith to come alongside you. As a parent, your connection to Christ and your connection to His church matters because you need the support of other believers.

The church can train you in God's Word and keep you accountable to the value of Scripture, prayer, devotion, service, and missions. The church can and should come alongside you as you raise the banner of those spiritual conditions in the lives of your kids too.

The world is screaming at you everyday to pursue your own desires and purpose your life based on what feels good to you. What believers must do is determine to submit to God and His desires instead. Ultimately, what feels good and desirable to a fully devoted Christ-follower is that which pleases the Lord.

In Exodus, in order to spare the lives of their firstborn children, parents were instructed to paint their door frames with blood. Blood on the doorposts was the distinguishing mark. The very next time that God's wanderers had doors of their own, blood wasn't the medium of choice. In Deuteronomy, in order to set the lives of their children in the right direction, parents were instructed to write the words of God on those door frames and on their gates, so that the commitment they made to the Lord was the last thing they saw on the way out of the house and the first thing they saw upon their return.

As parents, you can do this. Not alone. Not by your own power. But by the power of God flowing from a community of faith that He has purposed to be His hands and feet in the world until Christ's victorious return. Be bold and confidently convinced of the power you have in Jesus' name to parent well and raise kids who grow up to know and follow Him.

Stop punishing yourself for mistakes. Use your errors as a parent to your advantage as you model confession and repentance. Seek forgiveness first from God and then even from your children. Proverbs 26:11 is included in the canon of Scripture for a reason:

"As a dog returns to its vomit, so also a fool repeats his foolishness."

Maybe it's there just to make middle school boys laugh. Or perhaps, Proverbs 26:11 exists because when the God of this great universe wanted to paint a mental picture of what it means to repeat the same mistake over and over, He chose that of a dog enjoying dinner for the second time around. Silly? Maybe. Sick? Yes. Strategic? Absolutely.

Don't beat yourself up any longer for the good things you have neglected as a parent or the harmful things you might have engaged. Instead, learn from them and move on. This freedom is the transformative power of God's grace. You can start fresh and begin pursuing truths that will impact your children today.

As a mom, dad, or parental figure, you can elevate the value of Scripture in your own life and in your own home. You can model a love for God's Word and raise kids who understand the discipline it takes to regularly read it and follow what it says. You can be a faithful member of a local church that values Scripture. In doing so, you'll be far more adept at pointing out biblical principles and teaching scriptural truths to kids who can grow up in God's Word and not depart from it when they enter adulthood.

You can prioritize prayer and model for your children how to pray. You can demonstrate with your own dependence how vital your devotional life is to daily living. You can create family rhythms and set aside time for prayer and other habits, including tithing, so that God is a priority in every aspect of living, including but not limited to finances.

"GOD IS THE GOD OF 'RIGHT NOW.' HE DOESN'T WANT YOU SITTING AROUND REGRETTING YESTERDAY. NOR DOES HE WANT YOU WRINGING YOUR HANDS AND WORRYING ABOUT THE FUTURE. HE WANTS YOU FOCUSING ON WHAT HE IS SAYING TO YOU AND PUTTING IN FRONT OF YOU ... RIGHT NOW."
–PRISCILLA SHIRER

"If you desire not only to cope **but to thrive with vision and joy** as a parent, you need more than seven steps to solving whatever.

You need God's **helicopter view** of what he's called you to do. You need the gospel of Jesus Christ to reveal the foundational principles that will not only help you make sense of your task,

but will **change the way** you approach it."

–PAUL TRIPP

You can monitor family busyness and learn the art of saying "no" to some things, even good things, so that time engaged in the best things is protected. You can create a family margin so that serving and missions take a front seat in the life of your family.

As a mom, dad, parental figure, or church leader, you can leverage your influence and provide opportunities for kids to form friendships and build relationships with mentors who will lead them to Jesus.

As a parent, caregiver, or church leader, you can develop and foster a love for music that conveys theological truths and provides opportunities for private and family worship throughout the week. You can protect your children's minds from an onslaught of harmful messaging so prevalent in popular culture. You can do this, not in order to isolate them in fear, but to develop a love for holiness in them.

And regardless of whether or not your children are boys or girls or some of each, you can make a powerful investment in them that lasts. Whether or not you have an only child or a football team full of kids, God can use you to raise kids who are redeemed by His Son, filled with His Spirit, and who walk in His ways.

Ultimately, what you are doing as a parent is in fulfillment of Israel's primary command and Jesus' Great Commission. Repeating the words of God to your children, courtesy of God's communal instructing in Deuteronomy 6, is perhaps the greatest lesson. You are teaching them with word and deed, repeating the truths of God with your actions. Jesus' discipleship plan for the world was spelled out in some of His final words prior to ascending back to heaven. Matthew records them for us at the end of his Gospel:

"Go, therefore, and make disciples of all nations, baptizing them in the name of the Father and of the Son and of the Holy Spirit, teaching them to observe everything I have commanded you. And remember, I am with you always, to the end of the age" (Matthew 28:19-20).

We often view the Great Commission as singular call to go to the nations. Acts 1:8 reminds us that it starts right at home. Accompanying these final words in Matthew are these, recording a similar final conversation in Acts 1:8: *"But you will receive power when the Holy Spirit has come on you, and you will be my witnesses in Jerusalem, in all Judea and Samaria, and to the ends of the earth."*

Christ's Commission begins where we are, right at home. Starting with our own children, we can make disciples. That model includes teaching them to obey the Word of God. Perhaps that's why regular Bible reading didn't just register on our list of significant spiritual health predictors, but far exceeded every other ideal.

Research isn't intended to scare us, guilt us, or even challenge us. Well, maybe challenge us a little, in a healthy way. Primarily, the intention is to equip us with knowledge and insight. Take the data for what it's worth and make a plan.

You may be mentally devising a far-too-detailed plan about how you can conquer each and every one of the statistics offered by this research. You may be so overwhelmed by it all that you can't even begin. Simply go with Scripture and make regular Bible reading part of your own growth plan as well as your parental investment. Consider starting with the story of Jesus. Knock around the Gospels and read through Jesus' teachings. His lessons to the disciples and the crowds, and even the Pharisees, paint a gospel picture of God's redemptive grace that will serve us all well.

Jesus' final words in Matthew were a promise. He promised never to leave or abandon us. Ironically, shortly after that conversation, He did just that—He left the earth. But even though He is not currently with us in flesh and bone, He is even more present through the power of the Holy Spirit and His body, the church. Trust God's plan. Rely on God's Spirit and His church to give you the wisdom and the discernment to lead your family well.

ENDNOTES

1. LifeWay Research conducted the Nothing Less Study for LifeWay Kids. A demographically balanced online panel was used for interviewing American adults. The sample was screened to include only Protestant and non-denominational Christians who have a child (birth child, stepchild, adopted child, or foster child) between the ages of 18-30 and who attend religious services at least once a month. The survey was conducted September 22–October 5, 2016. Maximum quotas and slight weights were used for gender, region, age, ethnicity, and education to more accurately reflect the population. The completed sample of 2000 surveys provides 95% confidence that the sampling error does not exceed +2.3%. Margins of error are higher in sub-groups.

To measure the spiritual outcomes in the young adult children today, up to nine responses were combined to create a spiritual health score for each child as reported by the parent. Many characteristics of children and parenting practices have a significant relationship with the spiritual condition. However, many of these predictors may appear to have an impact on spiritual vitality only because they are correlated with other items that actually drive spiritual growth. To best answer the question of what drives spiritual growth, multiple linear regression was used to see if a significant relationship exists between each predictor and the spiritual health scale in the presence of the other significant characteristics.

Model selection was determined via stepwise selection using the Schwarz Bayesian Information Criterion (SBIC), which only includes significant terms and penalizes more complex models such that additional terms are only included if they provide substantial predictive improvement. Fifteen characteristics are predictive of spiritual health using model selection with multiple linear regression. These are divided into 3 tiers based on their relative importance in predicting the SCS. All comparisons presented are while holding other significant variables fixed. These characteristics explain 50% of the variability in spiritual condition score (R-Square of 0.5).

Because many of the characteristics most predictive of spiritual condition are about the child's habits growing up, relationships between parenting practices and positive spiritual outcomes are concealed. A second model was developed omitting the child items to better understand parenting

practices that predict a young adult's spiritual condition. Thirteen parenting characteristics are predictive of spiritual health using model selection with multiple linear regression. These characteristics explain 25% of the variability in spiritual condition score (R-Square of 0.5).

2. LifeWay Research, Parent Adventure Study, 2007-08.

3. LifeWay Research, Parent Adventure Study, 2007-08.

4. LifeWay Research, American Parental Characteristics Online Panel, 2013, http://www.lifeway.com/article/research-religious-convictions-not-among-most-desired-parent-traits.

5. LifeWay Research, Parent Adventure Study, 2007-08, http://www.lifeway.com/Article/LifeWay-Research-looks-at-role-of-faith-in-parenting.

6. LifeWay Research, KJV Study, 2011.

7. LifeWay Research, Transformational Discipleship Study, http://www.lifeway.com/Article/research-survey-bible-engagement-churchgoers.

8. LifeWay Research, Parent Adventure Study, 2007-08, http://www.lifeway.com/Article/LifeWay-Research-looks-at-role-of-faith-in-parenting.

9. LifeWay Research, Parent Adventure Study, 2007-08, http://lifewayresearch.com/2009/03/24/lifeway-research-looks-at-role-of-faith-in-parenting.

10. David Kinnaman and Gabe Lyons, *Good Faith* (Baker Books, 2016).

11. LifeWay Research, Parent Adventure Study, 2007-08, http://www.lifeway.com/Article/LifeWay-Research-looks-at-role-of-faith-in-parenting.

12. LifeWay Research, General Social Survey.

13. LifeWay Research, State of Theology Study, 2016, http://lifewayresearch.com/2016/09/27/americans-love-god-and-the-bible-are-fuzzy-on-the-details.

14. LifeWay Research, Nothing Less Study, 2016.

15. LifeWay Research, Nothing Less Study, 2016.

16. Eric Geiger, "Sharing the Word," *Facts & Trends*, https://factsandtrends.net/2017/06/26/sharing-the-word.

17. Thom Rainer, "How Do We Lead the People in Our Churches to Engage God's Word," *Facts & Trends*, July 3, 2017. https://factsandtrends.net/2017/07/03/how-do-we-lead-the-people-in-our-churches-to-engage-gods-word.

18. Daniel Im, "A New Way to Measure Discipleship," *Facts & Trends*, July 14, 2017, https://factsandtrends.net/2017/07/14/a-new-way-to-measure-discipleship.

19. LifeWay Research, Nothing Less Study, 2016.

20. LifeWay Research, Nothing Less Study, 2016.

21. LifeWay Research, Nothing Less Study, 2016.

22. LifeWay Research, Parenting Study, 2007-08.

23. LifeWay Research, Nothing Less Study, 2016.

24. Aaron Earls, "5 Simple Ways to Teach Kids Theology," *Facts & Trends*, February 9, 2015, https://factsandtrends.net/2015/02/09/5-simple-ways-to-teach-your-kids-theology.

25. LifeWay Research, Nothing Less Study, 2016.

26. Barna Research, *Transforming Children into Spiritual Champions* (Baker Books, 2016).

27. LifeWay Research, Nothing Less Study, 2016.

28. LifeWay Research, Nothing Less Study, 2016.

29. LifeWay Research, Nothing Less Study, 2016.

30. LifeWay Research, Nothing Less Study, 2016.

31. LifeWay Research, Nothing Less Study, 2016.

32. John Piper, "Tithing," September 10, 1995, http://www.desiringgod.org/messages/toward-the-tithe-and-beyond.

INFOGRAPHIC SOURCES

Page 12:
LifeWay Research, Parent Adventure Study, 2007-08, http://lifewayresearch. com/2009/03/24/parents-look-inward-not-upward-for-guidance.

Page 16:
LifeWay Research, American Parental Characteristics Online Panel, 2013, http:// www.lifeway.com/article/research-religious-convictions-not-among-most-desired-parent-traits.

Page 20:
LifeWay Research, Parent Adventure Study, 2007-08, http://www.lifeway.com/Article/ LifeWay-Research-looks-at-role-of-faith-in-parenting.

Page 23:
LifeWay Research, Parent Adventure Study, 2007-08, http://lifewayresearch. com/2009/03/24/parents-look-inward-not-upward-for-guidance.

Page 29:
LifeWay Research, Parent Adventure Study, 2007-08, http://lifewayresearch. com/2009/03/24/lifeway-research-looks-at-role-of-faith-in-parenting.

Page 30:
LifeWay Research, Parent Adventure Study, 2007-08.

Page 32:
David Kinnaman and Gabe Lyons, *Good Faith* (Baker, 2016).

Page 35:
LifeWay Research, Parent Adventure Study, 2007-08, http://www.lifeway.com/Article/ LifeWay-Research-looks-at-role-of-faith-in-parenting.

Page 36-37:
LifeWay Research, Nothing Less Study, 2016.

Page 50:
LifeWay Research, Nothing Less Study, 2016.

Page 53:
Brad Waggoner, *The Shape of Faith to Come: Spiritual Formation and the Future of Discipleship*, (Nashville: B&H, 2008), 275.

Page 54 (graphics 1 and 2):
LifeWay Research, King James Version Study, 2011.

Page 54 (graphic 3):
LifeWay Research, Transformational Discipleship Study, http://www.lifeway. com/Article/research-survey-bible-engagement-churchgoers.

Page 55:
LifeWay Research, American Views on Bible Reading, 2016, lifewayresearch.com/2017/04/25/ lifeway-research-americans-are-fond-of-the-bible-dont-actually-read-it.

Page 63:
LifeWay Research, Nothing Less Study, 2016.

Page 68:
Heron Associates, Inc. Bible Readership Focus Groups, October 17, 2014.

Page 72:
LifeWay Research, Transformational Discipleship Study. http://www.lifeway.com/Article/research-survey-bible-engagement-churchgoers

Page 73:
LifeWay Research, American Views on Bible Reading, 2016, http://lifewayresearch.com/2017/04/25/ lifeway-research-americans-are-fond-of-the-bible-dont-actually-read-it.

Page 74:
LifeWay Research, Transformational Discipleship Study. http://www.lifeway.com/Article/research-survey-bible-engagement-churchgoers

Page 75:
LifeWay Research, American Views on Bible Reading, 2016, http://lifewayresearch.com/2017/04/25/ lifeway-research-americans-are-fond-of-the-bible-dont-actually-read-it.

Page 77:
LifeWay Research, Nothing Less Study, 2016.

Page 78:
LifeWay Research, Spiritual Maturity Study, 2014. http://lifewayresearch.com/2013/02/21/ survey-spiritual-maturity-comes-through-intentionality.

Page 81:
LifeWay Research, Church Dropouts, 2007.

Page 83:
LifeWay Research, Nothing Less Study, 2016.

Page 85:
LifeWay Research, Nothing Less Study, 2016.

Page 87:
LifeWay Research, Nothing Less Study, 2016.

Page 89:
Barna Research, Short-Term Mission Trips, October 6, 2008. https://www.barna.com/research/despite-benefits-few-americans-have-experienced-short-term-mission-trips/

Page 93:
LifeWay Research, Nothing Less Study, 2016.

Page 95:
54. LifeWay Research, Nothing Less Study, 2016.

Page 99:
LifeWay Research, Nothing Less Study, 2016.

Page 101:
LifeWay Research, Millennials Prefer Experience, November 3, 2010. http://lifewayresearch.com/2010/11/03/ lifeway-research-finds-american-millennials-prefer-experience-over-expertise/

Page 105:
LifeWay Research, Nothing Less Study, 2016.

Page 111:
LifeWay Research, Nothing Less Study, 2016.

Page 113:
LifeWay Research, Sharing Faith Study, http://www.lifeway.com/Article/ research-survey-sharing-christ-2012

Page 114:
LifeWay Research, Spirital Maturity Study, http://www.lifeway.com/Article/ research-study-selflessness-leads-to-spiritual-maturity